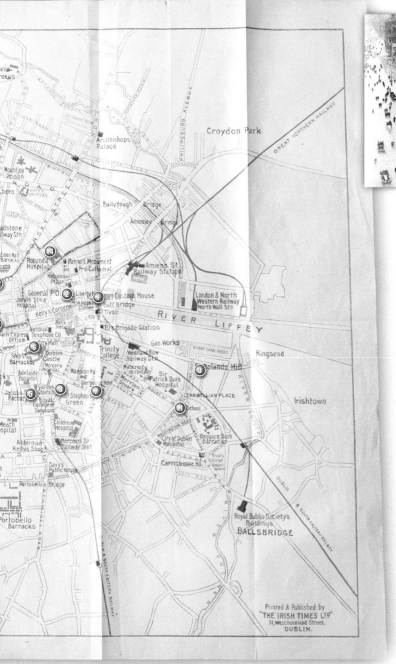

Nurse Elizabeth O'Farrell, walks with a white flag towards the British. Rebels are offered only unconditional surrender. At 3.30pm Pearse surrenders, and after the garrison says the rosary, they leave 16 Moore Street. At 3.45pm Pearse is taken before General Maxwell at the HQ of the Irish Command at Parkgate Street **(13)** and signs a general order of surrender.

Connolly countersigns surrender order, but only for men under his command in Moore Street and St Stephen's Green. Ned Daly is allowed to lead the march of his men from the Four Courts to the surrender point at the Gresham Hotel. The surrendered rebels are corralled on open ground behind Rotunda **(14)**, where they remain for the night.

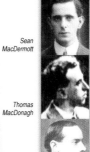

POSTSCRIPT

On Sunday, rebels at Boland's Mill, Jacob's Factory, St Stephen's Green, South Dublin Union and Marrowbone Lane surrender. They are abused by angry Dubliners. The prisoners are marched to Richmond Barracks **(15)**, where leaders are identified.

In the days and weeks that follow the surviving rebels are imprisoned and court-martialled. Executions begin. The seven signatories of the Proclamation of the Irish Republic, Patrick Pearse, Sean MacDermott, Thomas Clarke, Eamonn Ceannt, James Connolly, Thomas MacDonagh and Joseph Plunkett, are shot. Eight others are executed for taking part in the Rising, including Pearse's brother Willie. Many are deported to prisons in England and Wales, including Eamon de Valera, commander of the Boland's Mill garrison.

Normal life begins to resume, but the normality has changed. Public opinion, initially hostile to the rebels, begins to swing behind them as the leaders go to their deaths. In military terms the 2,000 men and women who had challenged the might of empire had failed. But as the poet WB Yeats observed, the result was that all was changed, "changed utterly".

James Connolly

Joseph Plunkett

Sean MacDermott

Thomas MacDonagh

Patrick Pearse

Thomas Clarke

Eamonn Ceannt

This map was published in a special
IRISH TIMES *"Handbook" after the Rising.*

fighting. There is a gun battle at the South Dublin Union. Crown troops use Guinness lorries as improvised armoured vehicles. Looting continues. In O'Connell Street, Clery's and the Imperial Hotel crash to the ground as the centre of Dublin burns.

Eamon de Valera under arrest

than 90 prisoners and captures four police barracks. At 8pm, a decision is made to evacuate a burning GPO.
Pearse, Connolly, Plunkett, Clarke and MacDermott halt in a house on Moore St, where they plan to make their way through back streets to

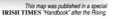

Friday April 28
General Maxwell arrives in the early hours, and issues a proclamation. A significant rebel assault on Ashbourne Co Meath takes place

Poster design: Francis Bradley, © IRISH TIMES STUDIO

AN ROINN
OIDEACHAIS AGUS EOLAÍOCHTA
DEPARTMENT OF EDUCATION AND SCIENCE
With thanks to the Department of Education & Science and The Irish Photographic Archive

THE IRISH TIMES BOOK OF THE 1916 RISING

SHANE HEGARTY & FINTAN O'TOOLE

GILL & MACMILLAN

Gill & Macmillan Ltd

Hume Avenue

Park West

Dublin 12

with associated companies throughout the world

www.gillmacmillan.ie

ISBN-13: 978 07171 4191 3

ISBN-10: 0 7171 4191 8

Index compiled by Cover to Cover

Print origination by Design Image

Printed by Butler & Tanner, Frome, Somerset

The paper used in this book is made from the wood pulp of managed forests. For every tree felled, at least one tree is planted, thereby renewing natural resources.

A CIP catalogue record is available for this book from the British Library.

CONTENTS

ACKNOWLEDGMENTS

The Irish Times wishes to thank the staff of the National Photographic Archive, a division of the National Library of Ireland, for sourcing illustrations, and the staff of the National Archives for their generous assistance. The National Museum of Ireland, the Gilbert Library and Military Archives also gave valuable assistance.

It is also grateful to John McGuiggan, who provided the authors with the witness account of Capt. A.A. Dickson and to Alex Findlater for the account by Capt. Harry de Courcy-Wheeler.

Much of this book was originally published as a special *Irish Times* supplement in March 2006.

The authors would like to thank, and acknowledge the invaluable role of that supplement's editor Kieran Fagan and designer Joe Breen. Substantial contributions were also made by Stephen Collins and Joe Carroll.

Joe Carroll contributed the following pieces to this book: 'How *The Irish Times* covered this "desperate episode"' and 'The Beginning of the End'.

Stephen Collins wrote: 'Who Were the Men Who Signed The Proclamation?' and 'What Were the Forces That Fought on Easter Week?'.

Kieran Fagan wrote: 'The Real Squalor in "Strumpet City"'.

Seamus Martin contributed: 'Brothers in Arms on Different Sides'.

Thanks also to Geraldine Kennedy, Gerry Smyth, Paddy Smyth and Peter Murtagh, for their editorial guidance and ideas during its compilation; and to Eoin McVey for his help in bringing the supplement from the newspaper and onto the book shelves.

PHOTO CREDITS

For permission to reproduce photographs the authors and publisher gratefully acknowledge the following:

2, 11, 162, 164, 180 © The Allen Library; 60, 61, 69, 98, 115, 131, 137, 149, 159, 174 © Camera Press Ireland; 197 © Corbis/ Bettmann; 7, 9, 16, 22, 54, 65, 70, 74, 89, 96, 116, 119, 122, 144, 146, 148, 177, 186, 188, 189, 192, 194 © Getty Images/ Hulton Archive; 24 © Getty Images/ Roger Viollet; 170 © The Illustrated London News Picture Library; 44, 176 © Kilmainham Gaol Collection; 56 © Mander & Mitchenson Theatre Collection; 73, 79, 198 © Mary Evans Picture Library; 30 © Military Archives; 27, 28, 29, 43, 48T, 48B, 49T, 66B, 85, 86, 90, 101, 106, 108, 135, 141, 147, 152, 200 © National Library of Ireland; 8, 15, 46 © National Museum of Ireland; 5, 35, 40, 51, 66T, 80, 83, 84, 105, 132, 153, 158, 163, 167, 181, 182 © RTÉ Stills Library; 3, 12, 19, 20, 50T, 50B, 68, 92, 102, 112, 123, 125, 126, 140, 150, 143, 168, 169, 178, 173, 185T, 185B © Topfoto.

Colour section: Images courtesy of *The Irish Times*; Kilmainham Gaol Collection; Mary Evans Picture Library; National Library of Ireland; Thomas Ryan, RHA; Topfoto.

Every effort has been made to trace all copyright holders, but if any has been inadvertently overlooked we would be pleased to make the necessary arrangements at the first opportunity.

PRELUDE

1913

JANUARY 16TH: HOME RULE BILL PASSED BY THE HOUSE OF COMMONS, AFTER DEFEAT OF EDWARD CARSON'S AMENDMENT TO EXCLUDE ULSTER.

JULY 15TH: HOME RULE BILL DEFEATED IN HOUSE OF LORDS.

AUGUST 18TH: WILLIAM MARTIN MURPHY LEADS DUBLIN EMPLOYERS IN LOCKING OUT WORKERS WHO REFUSE TO LEAVE IRISH TRANSPORT AND GENERAL WORKERS' UNION.

AUGUST 26TH: UNION LEADER JAMES LARKIN CALLS GENERAL STRIKE.

NOVEMBER 19TH: IRISH CITIZEN ARMY FORMED, INITIALLY TO PROTECT STRIKERS IN CONFRONTATIONS WITH THE POLICE.

NOVEMBER 25TH: IRISH VOLUNTEERS FORMED.

1914

JANUARY 18TH: LOCKOUT ENDS AS ITGWU ADVISES MEMBERS TO RETURN TO WORK.

MARCH 20TH–25TH: CURRAGH INCIDENT IN WHICH 57 BRITISH ARMY OFFICERS STATE THEIR UNWILLINGNESS TO COERCE ULSTER INTO HOME RULE.

APRIL 2ND: CUMANN NA MBAN FORMED AS WOMEN'S AUXILIARY TO IRISH VOLUNTEERS.

APRIL 24TH–25TH: ULSTER VOLUNTEERS LAND GUNS AT LARNE AND OTHER PORTS.

MAY 25TH: AMENDED HOME RULE PASSED IN HOUSE OF COMMONS.

JUNE 16TH: IRISH VOLUNTEERS ACCEPTS DEMAND OF IRISH PARTY LEADER JOHN REDMOND FOR 25 NOMINEES ON ITS PROVISIONAL COMMITTEE.

JULY 26TH: IRISH VOLUNTEERS LAND GUNS AT HOWTH.

AUGUST 3RD: GERMANY DECLARES WAR ON FRANCE.

AUGUST 4TH: GERMANY INVADES BELGIUM. UK DECLARES WAR ON GERMANY.

MID-AUGUST: THE SUPREME COUNCIL OF THE IRISH REPUBLICAN BROTHERHOOD DECIDES IN PRINCIPLE TO STAGE AN UPRISING BEFORE THE END OF THE WAR.

SEPTEMBER 15TH: SUSPENDING ACT DELAYS IMPLEMENTATION OF HOME RULE FOR ONE YEAR, OR UNTIL END OF WAR.

SEPTEMBER 18TH: GOVERNMENT OF IRELAND ACT ALLOWS FOR TEMPORARY EXCLUSION OF PARTS OF ULSTER FROM HOME RULE.

SEPTEMBER 20TH: JOHN REDMOND, AT WOODENBRIDGE, CALLS ON VOLUNTEERS TO FIGHT FOR UK IN THE WAR, CAUSING SPLIT.

DECEMBER 27TH: SIR ROGER CASEMENT SIGNS 'TREATY' IN BERLIN FOR THE ESTABLISHMENT OF AN IRISH BRIGADE IN GERMAN SERVICE.

1915

APRIL–JUNE: JOSEPH PLUNKETT UNDERTAKES A CLANDESTINE JOURNEY TO BERLIN TO TREAT WITH THE GERMANS.

LATE MAY: SUPREME COUNCIL OF IRB FORMS MILITARY COMMITTEE CONSISTING OF PATRICK PEARSE, JOSEPH PLUNKETT AND EAMONN CEANNT.

AUGUST 1ST: PEARSE DELIVERS MILITANT ORATION AT GRAVESIDE OF OLD FENIAN, JEREMIAH O'DONOVAN ROSSA.

DECEMBER: MILITARY COUNCIL OF IRB FORMED, WITH THOMAS CLARKE AND SEÁN MACDERMOTT JOINING PEARSE, PLUNKETT AND CEANNT.

THE REBELS

On the night of July 25th 1914, Andy O'Neill, a constable in the Dublin Metropolitan Police, had a strange dream. 'I dreamed,' he told his colleague Patrick Bermingham, 'that there were a lot of women praying for me in the sacristy of the chapel and I could see a stream of blood running down the street.' Bermingham remembered O'Neill's dream for a long time after. 'It was peculiar,' he recalled, 'that on that same day blood was spilled and was flowing down the street in Bachelor's Walk.'

Three months earlier, the Ulster Volunteer Force (UVF), which had vowed to fight Home Rule by all means necessary, had landed nearly 50,000 rifles and three million rounds of ammunition at Larne in Co. Antrim, and Bangor and Donaghadee in Co. Down. In

In July 1914, the yacht Asgard *sailed from Hamburg to Howth with 900 German Mauser rifles and 29,000 rounds of ammunition bound for the National Volunteers. En route, its owner, Erskine Childers, took this photograph of his wife, Mary, and her friend Mary Spring-Rice.*

The Asgard *guns arrive at Howth on July 26th 1914 and its cargo is brought ashore by the gathered National Volunteers as Erskine Childers (on the left in oilskins) looks on.*

response, the nationalist National Volunteers ran 900 German Mauser rifles and 29,000 rounds of ammunition into Howth on July 26th 1914. Since the authorities had turned a blind eye to the UVF's gun-running, it seemed likely that they would do the same in Dublin. Instead, troops of the King's Own Scottish Borderers, who had been sent to Howth in a failed attempt to stop the landing, were jeered and stoned by a crowd on Bachelor's Walk as they made their way back into the city. They opened fire and killed four people. It was the first sign that the conflict over Ireland's place in the United Kingdom, which had so long been conducted within the realms of parliamentary politics, could cause blood to flow on the streets.

A direct response to the Ulster Volunteer Force's landing of arms in Larne, Co. Antrim, the Howth gun-running was a bold and public move by the National Volunteers, with the arms arriving in daylight on a Sunday afternoon.

Within days, a far greater blood-letting had begun. The outbreak of the First World War seemed at first to put Ireland's internal troubles in the shade. The Home Rule Bill, which was to create an all-Ireland parliament, was suspended until the end of hostilities. The Ulster Unionist leader Edward Carson offered the UVF for service in the war and much of it was eventually incorporated into the 36th Ulster Division of the army. The Irish Parliamentary Party leader, John Redmond, matched the offer and urged members of the Irish Volunteers to serve in the British Army 'wherever the firing line extends'. When a more militant minority distanced itself from Redmond's line and protested that 'Ireland cannot, with honour or safety, take part in foreign quarrels otherwise than through the free action of a national government of her own', the Volunteers split and Redmond established his own National Volunteers.

The overwhelming majority stayed loyal to Redmond. British intelligence estimated that just 13,500 of the 188,000 Volunteers went with the militant faction led by Eoin MacNeill, its president and chief of staff, Bulmer Hobson, Michael O'Rahilly, Patrick Pearse, Thomas MacDonagh, Joseph Plunkett, Piaras Beaslaí, Eamonn Ceannt, Seán MacDermott and Liam Mellows – and that may have been an exaggeration of their strength. (More recent estimates range from 2,000 to 12,300.) Some of the militants actually welcomed the split, Patrick Pearse asserting that 'this small, compact, perfectly disciplined separatist force is infinitely more valuable than the unwieldy, loosely-held-together mixum-gatherum force we had before the split.'

By early 1916 there were about 146,000 Irishmen fighting in the Great War, and at most 15,000 members of the Irish Volunteers. Within that minority there was another minority:

Having landed the weapons at Howth, some of the 800 assembled National Volunteers bear arms and prepare to march into the city centre.

THE KIDNAPPING OF BULMER HOBSON

As the day of the planned Rising approached, tensions rose within the rebel ranks. Con O'Donovan, an agricultural science student who was originally from Cork, had planned to go home for the Easter holidays but instead spent Holy Week carrying dispatches and moving ammunition around Dublin. 'One night, after assisting in the removal of some ammunition to the house of Seán Tobin in Nelson Street, I was arrested by the said Seán as a G-man [a member of the intelligence branch of the DMP], ordered to give up my gun (I carried a .32 revolver) and imprisoned in the cellar where Garry Houlihan stood guard over me with a loaded automatic, until, at my request, they sent a messenger to the Keating Branch of the Gaelic League in North Frederick Street for someone to identify me. Gearóid O'Súilleabháin soon arrived, laughed them to scorn, and I was released ... I thought Tobin knew me and was disgusted at the mistake and the waste of time.'

Ironically, O'Donovan was subsequently sent to guard one of his erstwhile commanders. Bulmer Hobson was not just a senior figure in the IRB but one of the guiding lights of the whole Volunteer movement from its inception. He was also, however, an opponent of a rising without German help, and was regarded by the conspirators as being too influential and formidable to be left to his own devices. On Good Friday afternoon, they arrested him.

O'Donovan, who was initially detailed to guard the prisoner, was somewhat perplexed. 'Although I had implicit confidence in the men who detailed for me for these jobs, I was glad to find I was not left too long guarding that prisoner. Knowing what I did, and not knowing all, I found it hard to guess why Hobson should be a prisoner, but I gathered from him that what he felt most was the fact that he was not trusted.' O'Donovan wondered if the whole thing was not just a silly mistake: 'Had I not been arrested myself as a G-man? Possibly there was some mistake about him too, which would soon be rectified.' He was glad to be relieved of his task and 'consoled [himself] with the belief that the men who made him a prisoner knew what they were about.'

On Easter Saturday, Maurice Collins was given O'Donovan's job of guarding Hobson, who was now being held at the home of an activist, Martin Conlon. 'I was instructed to proceed with my rifle to Martin Conlon's house, Cabra Park, to take charge of Bulmer Hobson, who was detained there as a prisoner ... We found Hobson in a rather distressed state of mind and had to warn him several times to remain calm and quiet. He did not discuss the situation with us. Neither did he show any animosity towards us personally. While he was prisoner with us, his fiancée called inquiring if Bulmer Hobson were there, but we considered it better to deny his presence.'

Hobson's fiancée, Claire Gregan, was also his secretary at Volunteer headquarters, where, she recalled, 'there was great confusion in the building those days'. She had gone for lunch with Hobson on Good Friday and remembered that 'he mentioned Martin Conlon's house as a place where a meeting was to be held and that must have been why I went to look for him there when I heard that he was arrested. Naturally there was a lot of talk at the time and rumours were flying.' When she called to Conlon's house on Easter Saturday looking for Hobson, she felt that the Volunteer who answered the door (Maurice Collins) 'looked rather frightened' and felt sure that his denials were lies. 'Bulmer told me afterwards he heard me and made a move to come to the door and that another Volunteer who was guarding him pointed a gun at him ... I went away and Bulmer saw me going down to the gate. He was in the front room at the side of the hall.'

Early on Easter Sunday morning, Gregan went to Liberty Hall. She asked for James Connolly. 'I did not feel like tears but meant to insist as far as I could.' She asked where Hobson was. 'I said, "You know he has been arrested." He admitted that. I said, "Why was he arrested? Was he not a perfectly honest man?" He said he knew that but he might interfere with the plans for a rising. He was rather surly and I had to drag the words out of him. Connolly was rather like that.' She demanded that Connolly send Patrick Pearse out to her. 'He said much the same thing, but added that he would be all right. They knew, he said, that he would upset their plans, thinking the time was not ripe. He was quite nice and quite polite.'

Hobson, who had done more than anyone else to organise and lay out a strategy for a nationalist militia guided by the IRB, was held until Monday evening, when the Rising was well under way, and subsequently written out of the history of Irish republicanism.

After British troops tangled briefly with the Howth gun-runners, they were jeered and stoned by a crowd as they returned to the city. Firing on the crowd, they killed four people and injured 37. Dubliners turned out in great numbers for each of the funerals.

The Irish Volunteers held its first public meeting at the Rotunda in Dublin on November 25th 1914. Addressed by Eoin MacNeill, crowds filled the concert hall and spilled out into the grounds outside.

the 2,000 or so members of the secret, oath-bound Irish Republican Brotherhood, effectively controlled by the veteran nationalist Thomas Clarke and committed to staging a rebellion before the end of the Great War. There were also among the potential militants about 250 members of the Irish Citizen Army, initially formed during the great labour conflict of 1913 as a workers' defence force, but now, under James Connolly, increasingly committed to a nationalist uprising.

Unbeknownst to MacNeill, the IRB minority infiltrated itself into positions of power within the Irish Volunteers, with Pearse becoming Director of Military Organisation, Hobson Quartermaster General, Plunkett Director of Military Operations, MacDonagh Director of Training and Ceannt Director of Communications. The IRB also controlled the four Dublin battalions of the Volunteers, through their commandants MacDonagh, Ceannt, Ned Daly and Éamon de Valera.

The IRB militants themselves, however, were initially convinced that a rising could not take place without substantial German assistance. In a memorandum presented to the German government in Berlin by Joseph Plunkett and Roger Casement, they stated that it 'would be impossible to bring any considerable military operation to a successful issue without help from an external source'. They outlined a two-pronged strategy. The Volunteers would seize Dublin, capturing government officials, and disrupting administration, transport and communications. A German force of 12,000 men would be landed in the West of Ireland and, supported by a simultaneous western uprising, would take

Limerick and distribute 40,000 rifles. The combined German-Irish force would then defeat the British in Ireland, allowing Germany to establish naval bases on the west coast and use its U-boats to cut off Britain's vital sea routes in the Atlantic.

When Plunkett left Berlin in late June 1915, however, he did so without any concrete assurances from the Germans, who had no way of knowing whether Plunkett was merely a fantasist and who had seen the failure of Casement's attempts to raise an Irish Brigade from Irish prisoners held by Germany. Plunkett was given to understand, however, that German support might be forthcoming if the IRB set a definite date for a rising. This belief acted as a spur to the militants to begin serious preparations. Yet, by January 1916, when the decision was taken to fix the Rising for Easter 1916, the Volunteers as a whole had only 3,370 guns, including rifles, shotguns and revolvers.

Eoin MacNeill (right), pictured in 1923 with Douglas Hyde, founder of Conradh na Gaeilge and later President of the Irish Free State.

To make up for the deficit in arms, Plunkett had established a rough arms factory at his family property of Larkfield in the countryside at Kimmage to the south-west of Dublin. The small, eight-acre farm had become an unofficial headquarters for IRB activists in the Irish disapora in Britain, who were coming to Ireland to avoid conscription into the army. They were dubbed 'the Liverpool lambs', although many were from Glasgow or, as in the case of the young Michael Collins, London. Some crude bombs were manufactured at

Larkfield, and explosives and ammunition were stolen from the Arklow munitions factory and even in Scotland. Even so, it was clear that without German help, the would-be rebels would not have sufficient arms for a sustained military campaign against the British Army.

One of the more pressing fears of the IRB militants, moreover, was that their plans would be derailed by James Connolly and the Citizen Army, who seemed ready to stage a weak rebellion of their own, thus provoking a military crack-down by the authorities in which the IRB's own leadership would be rounded-up. Connolly was indeed planning his own armed uprising, believing that it could act as a catalyst for a wider revolution. The authorities, he reckoned, would over-react, and repression would create a more general backlash. This, he hoped, would generate a chain reaction in which an Irish revolution would spark a general European revolt against the war and the ruling classes. In the first issue of his paper, the *Irish Worker*, after the outbreak of the war, he had predicted that 'Ireland may yet set the torch to a European conflagration that will not burn out until the last throne and the last capitalist bond and debenture will be shrivelled on the funeral pyre of the last warlord.'

On the face of it, the IRB's plans for a German invasion of Ireland did not sit easily with Connolly's vision of a revolution against all of Europe's imperial powers. Unlike Pearse, Connolly found nothing glorious in the carnage of the Great War. In December 1915, when Pearse wrote (anonymously) that 'the old heart of the earth needed to be warmed by the red wine of the battlefields', Connolly dismissed the article as the work of a 'blithering idiot'. But his increasing impatience for action encouraged Connolly to join with anyone who would help him light the spark. In negotiations with Pearse, MacDermott and Plunkett beginning on January 19th 1916, he agreed to abandon his own plans for an insurrection, join the IRB's Military Council and plan a joint Citizen Army/ Volunteer rising for Easter.

Most Volunteers, including IRB members outside of the inner circle around Thomas Clarke, and even the IRB's own Supreme Council, by now had a sense that a rising was being contemplated but no clear notion of how and when it might happen. Desmond FitzGerald, for example, remembered that, 'Even now we did not fully envisage a rising. We probably thought of Germans landing in England and in Ireland, or of our making an alliance with them, and, when the war ended in England's defeat, and the Germans evacuated these islands, an Irish government would take control in Ireland, while England would settle down to the position of a minor power.'

Although short on both uniforms and weapons right up to the actual Rising, the Irish Volunteers did have a small number of both. These men were pictured at a training camp in 1915.

William Cosgrave, a Sinn Féin member of Dublin Corporation and a lieutenant in the Volunteers summed up the feelings of many activists. 'I met Thomas MacDonagh early in the Spring of 1916 when he spoke of a rising within the next month or two, and went on to express a desire to hear my views. I told him it would be little short of madness – as we lacked men and munitions. While there had been some expansion in Volunteer recruiting throughout the country, Dublin did not share in the increase to any great extent. MacDonagh enquired as to whether my opinion would be affected by such developments as a German naval victory, neutralisation of the British fleet by submarines, importation of arms on a large scale, the landing in Ireland of the 69th Regiment [a largely Irish unit of the US army]. I agreed that developments such as these would completely alter the situation – that the Volunteers alone were not capable of a sustained conflict. I was not impressed with gaining a moral victory.'

Patrick Pearse, right, was a Gaelic revivalist and schoolmaster, who was among the Irish Republican Brotherhood leaders to infiltrate the Irish Volunteers. He was commander-in-chief of the rebels during Easter week. Pictured here with his brother Willie, both would be executed following the Rising.

A majority of the leadership of the Irish Volunteers remained convinced, likewise, that a rising without significant aid from Germany would be folly. The militants had to deceive their own official leader, Eoin MacNeill. MacNeill's position was that the Volunteers should resist, by force if necessary, any attempt to disarm them, but that aggressive action could not be contemplated unless it had a real chance of success. On April 5th, Patrick Pearse met MacNeill and 'explicitly repudiated the suggestion that he or his friends contemplated insurrection'. A few days later, MacNeill again confronted Pearse, who now confirmed that a rising was imminent and that the Volunteers had long been under the secret control of the IRB.

MacNeill, bolstered by Bulmer Hobson, then issued a command to the Volunteers that 'all orders of a special character issued by Commandant Pearse with regard to military movements of a definite kind' were 'hereby recalled or cancelled'. He wavered during Holy Week, believing that Roger Casement's arms shipment from Germany *(see panel, page 19)* would arrive and that some kind of defensive manoeuvre by the Volunteers might be necessary. A forged 'Castle document', detailing plans by the authorities to suppress the Volunteers and arrest hundreds of Catholic and nationalist leaders (including the Archbishop of Dublin) bolstered his willingness to allow preparations for armed resistance. When the news came that Casement's expedition had failed, and when he learned that the 'Castle document' was largely a fake, he decided that he had to act to prevent manoeuvres that had been scheduled for Easter Sunday, and which he now realised were a cover for the Rising. Late on Easter Saturday, he went to the office of the *Irish Independent* to place an order that 'no parades, marches or other movements of the Irish Volunteers will take place' in the following day's *Sunday Independent*. On Sunday, Michael O'Rahilly drove south to take MacNeill's orders to the Munster units of the Volunteers.

For James Connolly's family, who had finally made a reasonably decent life for themselves in Belfast after years of poverty, the first stirrings of the Rising were manifested in the break-up of the home they had worked so hard to establish. His wife Lily was instructed to leave Belfast and make her way to a bare cottage in the Dublin Mountains owned by Countess Markievicz. Ina, Connolly's daughter, recalled the scene: 'Sadly, mother looked around the home that she cherished; here she was leaving all the convenience of modern life and the work of the last five years which it took to build up, to go to an empty cottage on the hills of Dublin, miles away from anyone she knew. But she would carry out the wishes of her husband. She left Belfast very downhearted with the feeling that once again her hopes of a happy home had been dashed to the ground.'

For young Volunteers like Con O'Donovan, there was tension. 'One of these days of Holy Week, I was set, with Tommy O'Connor, to watch movements around the Castle Yard and Lower Castle Gate, and I think if I had been alone I would have funked it. Not that Tommy was with me all the time. He must have been at least two hours away, in one stretch, on a report to Liberty Hall. Such a job was quite new to me, and the strain of endeavouring to move innocently in Dame Street, around that gate, was worse than being in [a] fight ... And then, what was I to report as unusual movement? At any rate, nothing unusual occurred, as far as I could see. Soldiers and police passed in and out, singly and in pairs, but there was no bustle, and when I found some of these "observing" me, I began to feel guilty, moved round the corner, and walked on a bit among the usual groups of passers-by.'

THE AUTHORITIES

As early as September 1914, the authorities at Dublin Castle had warnings that militant nationalists would attempt to stage an armed insurrection during the war. The DMP chief commissioner wrote to the under-secretary, pointing to Dublin as the likely source of danger, and predicting that, in the event of a rising, even followers of John Redmond might revolt: 'There is no doubt that so far as Dublin is concerned, the majority of the National Volunteers would follow the lead of the extreme section and hints have been given that they are not without hope of being able to assume and establish control of the Government of Ireland before the present difficulties are over and that they may attempt some escapade before long.' The following month, the Detective (G) Division of the DMP gave the under-secretary notes of speeches made at the first Irish Volunteers convention, predicting rebellion and bloodshed 'in the great fight for Ireland against the British Empire'. On April 7th 1916, when the Volunteers staged anti-recruitment public meetings in the city that were replete with violent rhetoric, the chief commissioner recommend firm action: 'The Sinn Féin party is gaining in numbers, in equipment, in discipline, and in confidence, and I think drastic action should be taken to limit their activities. The longer this is postponed, the more difficult it will be … ' Yet no real effort to disarm the Volunteers was ever made.

Arthur Hamilton Norway, an Englishman who arrived in Ireland in September 1912 as secretary of the Post Office, was struck by the reluctance of his fellow members of the Irish Administration to risk a confrontation with nationalist opinion. He viewed the chief secretary Augustine Birrell as 'a shrewd literary critic, but a negligent and undiscerning politician, who did not occupy his Lodge in Phoenix Park, and visited Ireland rarely.' He regarded all of those responsible for security in Ireland, with the exception of the head of the DMP Sir John Ross, as 'dominated by the strong conviction held by Mr Birrell, and adopted as a principle of action by the Ministry, that Ireland must be governed according to Irish ideas, by which doctrine they understood that all strong action must be foregone, and everything avoided which might conceivably create friction.'

For the day-to-day rulers of Ireland – Birrell and the under-secretary Sir Matthew Nathan – the most pressing issue was the recruitment of Irish soldiers to the war effort. They

Patrick Pearse, seen here speaking to a gathering at Dublin's Dolphin's Barn in 1915, welcomed the split between the Volunteers, believing that a small, disciplined force would be better than 'the unwieldy, loosely-held-together mixum-gatherum force we had before'.

knew very well that the Irish Volunteers and the Citizen Army were committed, at least in principle, to an uprising, but they also feared that any attempt to disarm them could lead to bloodshed and undermine nationalist support for the war. 'Action against these Volunteers', said Nathan, 'would have resulted in the alienation of the great bulk of the Irish people, which was not in favour of these people.' They were also inured to the sight of military displays. Even when, in October 1915, the Citizen Army under James Connolly and Constance Markievicz staged what seemed to some a mock attack on Dublin Castle, Nathan's response was phlegmatic: 'Of course, we were accustomed to all sorts of operations in Ireland.' As one observer, Kathleen Tynan, remarked, the very openness of the militants' armed displays tended to suggest that there was no secret plot: 'how could anyone believe in the seriousness of a conspiracy that so flaunted itself?'

Chief Secretary for Ireland, Augustine Birrell, who feared that any attempt to disarm the Volunteers could lead to bloodshed and undermine nationalist support for the war.

Birrell also felt that it would be impossible to disarm the Irish Volunteers without also taking action against the Redmondite National Volunteers and the Ulster Volunteers. 'The misery of the whole thing was this – you had armed bodies of Volunteers all over the place ... and if you could have got disarmament all round it would have been a blessing, but to disarm any one section of the population on the evidence that we had appeared to me to be a very dangerous and doubtful proposition.' Birrell was, nevertheless, increasingly anxious. He felt that 'Ireland lives under the microscope' and that the daily intelligence reports that flowed into Dublin Castle gave a good picture of the political situation. He also read the signs of the Dublin streets: 'The impression I got, walking around the streets, was that Sinn Féinism was in a certain sense in possession.'

Birrell's impressions produced few results, however. Hamilton Norway felt that the root of the problem was official complacency in London. 'It was indeed a chief difficulty of the situation that Irish disloyalty was not taken seriously in London, where it was usual to speak of it with contempt as displaying the characteristics of a comic opera ... Everyone believed that the point was off the Irish pikes, and the gunmen had forgotten how to shoot. That was partly true. But it was also true that dangerous men and organisations were stirring in their sleep, while those who should have watched them played golf and dined in peace.'

Norway attempted to purge his own staff at the Irish Post Office (which employed 17,000 people) of known IRB activists, but was largely frustrated by a mixture of English complacency and Irish defiance. On the one hand 'I had still to convince my chief and colleagues in London that there was danger in the situation, and this they refused resolutely to admit, telling me I had let myself be frightened by heady police officers and soldiers, and that no movement in Ireland need cause a moment's anxiety. Strong Unionists were as contemptuous as Liberals. All alike scouted the idea that Ireland could give serious trouble, and in this view my apprehensions and suggestions broke idly and spent themselves in vain.'

On the other hand, Norway's attempts to warn off militant members of his staff tended to be met with protestations of injured innocence. A few weeks before the Rising broke out, he approached a clerk, Con Collins, who was an IRB activist, to warn him of the consequences to his career of continuing 'his association with disloyal organisations'. 'Collins at once began to fence with me. "What are these associations?", he asked indignantly. "I specify none," I answered. "I warn you in terms which are quite general, and it is for you to interpret them, remembering that the warning is meant seriously and that this is wartime." "But evidently", he insisted, "you mean that I must drop my connection with the Gaelic Athletic Association. May I not take an interest in Irish sport?"' Just a few weeks later, Collins was in Kerry helping to oversee the arrangements for the hoped-for landing of German arms.

On Easter Saturday, Norway's son Nevil (afterwards famous as the novelist Nevil Shute) came to his father's office at the GPO to say that 'he did not like the look of things in Dublin, and would be happier about me if I were armed. Accordingly, he induced me to take from my safe the Colt Automatic which my son Fred used in the few weeks of splendid service which preceded his mortal wound near Armentieres. He cleaned it, charged the magazine and four other clips, and laid the whole in a short drawer of my desk, saying, "Now you have thirty shots, and I feel happier about you."'

Nevil Norway's suspicions were shared, with a great deal more concrete support, by British naval intelligence, which had broken German radio codes and was therefore able, in effect, to listen in on what the rebel conspirators were telling their German allies. The navy, however, was determined at all costs not to let the Germans know that the codes had been broken, and did not trust Dublin Castle to keep such crucial secrets. Its warnings thus tended to be discreet. On March 22nd, however, it did send a top-secret dispatch with the information from an 'absolutely reliable source' that the rebel leaders had decided to launch their insurrection by April 22nd.

CRIME AND THE BOTTLE

People of the early 20th century were as concerned about crime and drunkenness as they are now. In 1910, the national average for crimes including rape and murder was 21.02 per 10,000. In Dublin, this rose to 100 per 10,000. Meanwhile, when 22 Dublin pubs were watched for a two-week period, it was reported that 46,574 women and 27,999 children frequented the bars during that time. As Tim Pat Coogan points out in his book *1916: The Easter Rising*, this was 'not merely because most of them sold groceries as well. Insanity frequently caused by drinking methylated spirits or turpentine was estimated at 63.5 per thousand'.

Yet Augustine Birrell was not in Dublin at Easter. He had gone to London for a Cabinet meeting and decided to stay for the holiday period. He left, even though Dublin Castle had received naval intelligence on April 18th that a ship accompanied by two German submarines and carrying arms was heading for Ireland and that a rising was planned for Easter Saturday. The intelligence came with a warning that it might not be accurate, but since the first part of it proved to be true, it might have been logical to assume that a rising really was imminent.

Instead, the news of the capture of Roger Casement which reached Dublin Castle on the Friday evening (April 21st), created an assumption that, if a rising really was planned, it would not now go ahead. Senior officials tended to take the view that Casement, as an international celebrity, would have been the leader of any putative rebellion, and that the conspiracy had therefore been decapitated. The army commander Major Gen. L.B. Friend decamped to London for the long weekend on Friday evening, after hearing of Casement's arrest. He called in to the War Office in London on Saturday morning and was told of the scuttling of the arms ship. 'I was within touch with the Irish headquarters and I waited, of course, on Saturday, to hear of anything likely to occur.'

No military preparations were put in place for whatever was likely to occur: there were, in Dublin, just 400 troops in a state of 'immediate readiness'. At Dublin Castle, the guard consisted of just six soldiers, with around 20 in the nearby Ship Street Barracks. Large numbers of officers were given weekend leave, with many of those in Dublin planning to attend the races at Fairyhouse on Monday. No special orders were issued for dealing with the planned Volunteer manoeuvres on Easter Sunday.

SIR ROGER CASEMENT

On April 15th 1916, Sir Roger Casement, who had been in Germany on a failed mission to recruit Irish prisoners of war for a rising in Ireland, set sail from Wilhelmshaven in a German U-boat bound for Tralee Bay. The submarine was to rendezvous off the Kerry coast with a cargo ship, the *Libau*, which had left Hamburg on March 30th. En route, it was disguised as a Norwegian steamer, the *Aud*, complete with deceptive sea charts, logs, canned food and a cargo of pots and pans. It also carried 20,000 rifles, ten machine guns and a million rounds of ammunition. Casement, who had been strongly opposed to the idea of a rising without a substantial German military involvement, had decided after all to go back to Ireland and join an insurrection he knew to be planned for Easter Sunday.

Casement – with the assistance of the Irish Volunteer chief instructor, Capt. Robert Monteith – had been embarrassed by the attempt to set up a brigade from among the thousands of Irish then housed in German camps.

Sir Roger Casement's attempts to recruit rebels from among the Irish languishing in German POW camps proved unsuccessful. A handful volunteered, including those pictured, and were given uniforms and training by the Germans. But with relations strained as the Germans lost interest in supporting a rising, Casement's Brigade was disbanded.

'He was a tall gentleman,' remarked the police officer who apprehended Roger Casement. 'He looked foreign to me and not generally the type one meets in the street.'

Among the few to be impressed by their overtures was Maurice Meade, a Limerick man who had been a member of the First Expeditionary Force that landed in France at the start of the war, but had been captured in 1915. 'It must have been some time coming up to Christmas of 1915 that some German officers came along and called for all Irishmen to stand out. It was announced that all the Irishmen were to be sent home in time for Christmas. This was how they sorted out the Irishmen among the prisoners from the others, we were all sent to a new camp.'

At this new camp, Limburg, Casement addressed the Irish prisoners, appealing to them to strike a blow for their motherland. Only 56 agreed to join the Brigade, which was to be trained and sent to assist the rebellion in Ireland. Meade was among them. 'After Casement and Monteith had left, the German NCOs came around the hut to take the names of those who were willing to join the Irish Brigade. They were assisted in this by Keogh, Quinslink and Beverly, three fellow-prisoners of ours, whom apparently Casement had made contact with and were trusted by him to help in the formation of the Brigade.

'Soon after that, Keogh, Quinslink and Beverly went to Berlin where they were fitted with a new uniform that was specially designed and made for the Irish Brigade and they came back to the camp to show it to us. It was lovely uniform and looked very well. I wore such a uniform myself later and I also went to Berlin where we were presented to the Kaiser who came around and shook hands with each of us.'

The Brigade was trained by German soldiers, often in the use of captured British weapons about which the Irish pupils were generally more familiar than their teachers. Relations were strained. At one point, Casement and Monteith had to intervene when a row broke out between the Irish and Germans during which the Irish stole rifles, retreated to a hut and refused to allow any Germans in. Only when detentions were handed out to men on both sides was the mutiny resolved.

The Germans soon lost interest in the Irish Brigade and any large-scale support of a rising. Meade was present when Casement admitted failure. 'Shortly before Casement left Germany for Ireland, he again came to see us and addressed us. He pointed out that, though he had hoped that an effective fighting Brigade might have been built up in Germany to go to Ireland, now the Brigade was too small to go there but that we could give useful service elsewhere. For, he said, a shot fired for Ireland's freedom in Egypt could be as good as a shot fired in Ireland, encouraging us to volunteer for service for the German expeditionary forces in the Mediterranean.'

Meade was indeed encouraged, and this soldier who had begun the war on the British side ended it with a six-month spell fighting the British in Egypt.

Casement, Monteith and the Irish Brigade's Sgt Beverly (also known as Daniel Bailey) were aboard the German U-boat planning to rendezvous with the *Libau/Aud* at Tralee. The ship dropped anchor off Inishtooskert Island in Tralee Bay on Thursday, April 20th. At midnight, the submarine reached the rendezvous point just north-west of the island. The two boats, however, failed to make contact with each other either that night or during the clear daylight of Good Friday. The Irish Volunteers who were expected to be on the shore to signal to the German boats failed to materialise, as they believed they were not due until later that week.

The three Irishmen climbed into a collapsible dinghy during the early hours of Good Friday, and despite being tossed from it in the heavy surf they managed to make their way to Banna Strand.

Bernard Reilly, an RIC constable at Ardfert, Co. Kerry, was on duty on Friday morning when word came through that a boat had been found floating on the edge of the tide and 'that there were several articles in the boat which gave him the impression that somebody had landed.' There had also been reports of men acting suspiciously in the locality.

A sergeant and constable retrieved the boat and found, according to Constable Reilly, three Mauser pistols and two packets of ammunition. They also found signalling lamps, a small map showing a sketch of the coast and some other maps and papers.

Reilly, meanwhile, was searching around a place called McKenna's Fort when a man emerged from the shrubbery. 'He was a tall gentleman. He looked foreign to me and not generally the type one meets in the street. There was nothing unusual about his clothes. He wore a beard and had a more or less aristocratic appearance. I don't remember that his clothes were wet at that stage. He came towards me. I think I said "good morning" or "good day". I asked, "What are you doing here?" He replied, "Have I not a right to be here?"'

The man was Sir Roger Casement, although at first he insisted that he was Richard Morton, an Englishman who had arrived in the area to research a book on St Brendan. However, Reilly noticed that he kept pulling at the sword-stick he was carrying and seemed to be looking over his shoulder as if searching for others. 'I was carrying a rifle without ammunition,' remembered Reilly. 'I gave him to understand that if he was going to draw the sword I was going to fire the rifle.'

After Casement was identified by a local woman as one of three men she had seen coming from the direction of the sea while she was milking her cows early that morning, Casement was taken to the police barracks. During the journey some coded documents were found on him.

In the meantime, two Volunteers, Austin Stack and Con Collins, had been spotted in the locality. Having too late realised that the German boat had arrived, they searched for Casement until Collins was stopped and arrested. Stack managed to rescue him from the RIC station, only for Collins to later be re-arrested. Stack was also arrested before the end of the day.

The disaster got worse when three insurgents – Con Keating, Charles Monaghan and Donal Sheehan – who had been sent from Dublin to seize wireless equipment in Caherciveen and make radio contact with the German ships, drove off Ballykissane pier in the dark and drowned. The driver was the only survivor. Having lost sight of another car he was supposed to follow, he had taken a wrong turn and only realised his mistake when the headlamps shone on water.

At 6pm on Saturday evening, the *Libau*, still drifting around the Blasket Islands, was captured by two British sloops. Its captain had already managed to bluff his way out of trouble once before, but was not so successful a second time. The British vessels escorted the *Libau* to Queenstown (now Cobh), where its captain scuttled his ship, ending German involvement in plans for the Rising.

Thousands attend the funeral of Roger Casement, after his remains were repatriated from England in 1965. He had led the failed mission to land arms at Kerry on the eve of the Rising and was hanged for high treason.

THE UNEASY CALM BEFORE THE STORM

Sunday, April 23rd

- MANOEUVRES BY THE IRISH VOLUNTEERS AND THE CITIZEN ARMY, PLANNED AS A COVER FOR THE BEGINNING OF THE RISING, ARE CANCELLED BY THE VOLUNTEER CHIEF OF STAFF, EOIN MACNEILL.

- LARGE NUMBERS OF REBELS GATHER IN DUBLIN AND AROUND THE COUNTRY, BUT THERE IS DEEP CONFUSION ABOUT WHAT IS TO HAPPEN.

- THE REBEL LEADERS DECIDE TO POSTPONE THE RISING UNTIL NOON ON MONDAY.

- EXPLOSIVES ARE STOLEN BY THE REBELS AND STORED IN LIBERTY HALL.

- THE AUTHORITIES DISCUSS A PLAN TO RAID LIBERTY HALL AND ARREST AND DEPORT THE REBEL LEADERS, BUT DECIDE TO PUT OFF ACTION UNTIL MONDAY AT THE EARLIEST.

- ON THE WESTERN FRONT, THE BATTLE OF VERDUN, WHICH HAS BEEN RAGING SINCE LATE FEBRUARY, IS NOW IN ITS THIRD BLOODY PHASE, WITH THE FRENCH ARMY TRYING TO HOLD OFF ANOTHER MASSIVE GERMAN OFFENSIVE. BY MID-DECEMBER, WHEN THE BATTLE ENDS WITH NO ADVANTAGE GAINED BY EITHER SIDE, THERE WILL BE ALMOST A MILLION CASUALTIES, HALF OF THEM FATAL.

Around midnight, as Easter Saturday became Easter Sunday, Con O'Donovan went to Liberty Hall with a dispatch for James Connolly. 'The door was barred and an armed guard admitted and led me right up to Connolly where he lay on a mattress in a fairly large room, among perhaps thirty of his men, all lying down for the night, each with his rifle beside him.' As he left, O'Donovan was struck by the fact that many of these Citizen Army members who were preparing to fight for Ireland were slum dwellers with little to gain: 'I asked myself, "What impulse urges these men to fight?" Certainly not the hope that they will get anything out of it. What have they to fight for? A country. Yes, but how much of it? A room or two in a tenement.'

William Cosgrave, a Sinn Féin member of Dublin Corporation and a lieutenant in the Volunteers, summed up the feelings of many activists when he told Thomas MacDonagh that a rising would be 'little short of madness – as we lacked men and munitions'.

At five in the morning on Easter Sunday, Connolly's daughters Ina and Nora arrived in Dublin by train from Portadown. On the way to Liberty Hall Ina couldn't wait to see their father and started to run, but Nora called her back: 'You don't know who is watching you; they will get suspicious at you making a bolt for the Hall so early in the morning.' They got into the Hall but the guards were reluctant to wake their father, who had just gone to bed. When they were allowed into his room, they found him 'on a bed in a half-sitting position, his head resting on his hand'.

The previous day, at Coalisland, where the northern Volunteers were assembling, Nora and Ina Connolly had got the orders from Dublin cancelling the manoeuvres. 'This was a terrible blow,' remembered Ina, 'What did it mean? What could we do?' The women had decided to go to Dublin and at Portadown station they met one of the Belfast contingents, still heading for Coalisland. They suggested that the men should join them and go to Dublin 'but this they would not do; their orders were to take the men to Coalisland and this they would do, even though they were accompanied all the way by detectives.'

Nora and Ina travelled through the night to see their father. They told him of the failure of the northern mobilisation and he said 'This is a very serious situation.' He sent Ina to the Metropole Hotel to find Joseph Plunkett and give him the news.

When Ina got back to Liberty Hall, her father was up and dressed. For the first time, she saw him in his uniform. 'How splendid he looked! How pleased I was to see him in the uniform of Ireland's green!' He sent her out on a bicycle to see if there were unusual numbers of police or detectives on the streets. There were not. In spite of the capture of Roger Casement and the well-publicised Volunteer and Citizen Army manoeuvres planned for Easter Sunday, the authorities seemed to have no special contingency plans in place. The under-secretary Sir Matthew Nathan had written to the chief secretary Augustine Birrell on Saturday to say that 'I see no indications of a rising.'

On Easter Sunday, however, Nathan and the lord lieutenant, Lord Wimborne, learned that five 50lb cases of dynamite had been stolen from a quarry at Brittas, Co. Wicklow that morning, and that the police believed it had been taken to Liberty Hall. Wimborne and Nathan discussed the situation with military and police officials at the Vice Regal Lodge in Phoenix Park, with Wimborne urging an immediate raid on Liberty Hall and the arrest and deportation of the militant leaders.

'His Excellency', recalled Major Ivor Price of the Royal Irish Constabulary, 'wanted to rush Liberty Hall for the purpose of getting back the 250lbs of dynamite. The proposal was that 100 soldiers and 100 policemen should rush the Hall.' But Price argued that 'the leaders would not be there. Probably 100 lives would have been lost, and then the press would come down and say "Nothing was going to happen; you should not have interfered with them; it is Bachelor's Walk again."' Wimborne eventually agreed that the operation should be postponed at least until Monday, when the leaders would probably be at Liberty Hall and the military could be properly prepared. 'It was no good to stir up the hornet's nest', he concluded, 'unless they could capture the hornets.'

The hornet's nest was in reality well-occupied: both the would-be leaders of the Rising and many of their followers were there, most of them in a state of extreme agitation. Helena Molony, the official proprietor of James Connolly's newspaper the *Workers' Republic*, had been waiting for something to happen. For months she had been reading the cautious pronouncements of Eoin MacNeill and his ally Bulmer Hobson with disdain. 'We were to be cautious, we must not play the enemy's game, we must have no more forlorn hopes, "our children's children would vindicate Ireland's right to freedom", etc, etc. This provoked a storm of angry sarcasm, at least from us women. Our unfortunate young men friends were greeted with "Hello, here come the leaders of posterity, how were they when you saw them last?", or "Are your children's children punctual at their drill?" Mary Perolz [a Citizen Army stalwart] dubbed them the "fan go fóills" (wait-a-whiles), which name became general.'

THE REAL SQUALOR IN 'STRUMPET CITY'

The 1911 census records 62,365 families living in Dublin city. The average number in each family was 4.6, with an average of 8.6 people living in each house. The overall population stood at 304,802. The city was smaller then, effectively contained in the area between the Royal and Grand canals. Many better-off families lived in the suburbs, and do not appear in the city figures.

The housing stock was poor. Almost 50,000 families, or 75 per cent of families, lived in accommodation of less than five rooms. Breaking down that figure reveals a very bleak picture. Some 40 families lived in a shared room. About one-third of family units were slightly better off, having a room of their own. About 20 per cent of families lived in just two rooms.

There were 3,604 tenements in Dublin city in 1911. In them, there were 643 instances in which more than seven people lived in one room, 45 cases where there were 10 to a room, 16 with 11, and five where 12 or more lived in the one room. The squalor described in James Plunkett's novel *Strumpet City* was real.

A Housing Inquiry in 1914 made efforts to deal with the problem, but little local authority accommodation was provided during the First World War (1914–1918). The situation may have been marginally better in 1916 than that reported by the 1911 census, but it is fair to say that it was little changed from 1913, when Dublin's chief medical officer, Sir Charles Cameron, wrote: 'In the case of one room tenements, the occupants are usually very poor and unable to pay for more accommodation ... the wages of an unskilled labourer are rarely more than £1 per week.' Sir Charles noted that a tradesman, a tailor known to him living in Dame Court, could only earn 10 shillings a week, a quarter of which went on rent. His wife had to feed the family out of the balance, which meant they often went hungry.

Nurse Magrane made 269 visits to TB patients in their homes on the north side of Dublin city in April 1916. During the month, the city's Charles Street tuberculosis dispensary, close to Ormond Quay, was notified of 55 new northside cases to add to the existing caseload of 567. Her colleague, Nurse McKenna, visited a further 153 TB patients.

On the south side of the city the existing caseload was not so heavy at 537, but 44 new cases were notified in April, and nurses Considine and Murray visited 456 patients in their south city homes. Some 10 TB patients died in April, 10 houses were declared insanitary, and 26 reported for disinfection. Their work was disrupted when the military authorities took possession of the clinic, remaining in occupation until May 1st, when the premises had to be disinfected before reopening for business.

The position regarding literacy was more encouraging. Almost 250,000 of the population of the city was over nine years of age, and 92.6 per cent of them were able to read and write. The 1911 census was the first to measure literacy in this age group, so no comparison is possible.

However, it did show that the percentage of those of aged five and upwards unable to read and write had been dropping steadily. And just 3.9 per cent of the city's population said they could speak Irish in 1911, up from 3.3 per cent in 1901, but that must surely have risen by 1916, given the renewed interest in Gaelic culture.

SUNDAY
23
MONDAY
24
TUESDAY
25
WEDNESDAY
26
THURSDAY
27
FRIDAY
28
SATURDAY
29

Poole Street, Dublin, around 1910. The 1911 census records that the overall population stood at 304,802, with the average number in each family at 4.6, and an average of 8.6 people living in each house.

She was at Liberty Hall on Easter Sunday morning. 'I saw Eoin MacNeill's countermanding order in the paper and heard the discussion in Liberty Hall. Connolly was there. They were all heartbroken, and when they were not crying, they were cursing. I kept thinking, "Does this mean that we are not going out?" There were thousands like us ... Many of us thought we would go out single-handed, if necessary.'

Among the rank-and-file of the Volunteers, though, Con O'Donovan noted decidedly mixed feelings. 'One thing that stands out in my mind is the feeling of relief some men

A view down Sackville Street, as it was known in 1916, before the Rising. Nelson's Pillar is the tall building further down the street, with Daniel O'Connell's statue to the fore.

showed that day, as a result of the "manoeuvres" being called off by J. McNeill, while others were thoroughly disgusted.' O'Donovan himself was sent to Liberty Hall on Easter Sunday morning with a dispatch for Seán MacDermott 'but would not be admitted to his presence as he was, with the other signatories of the proclamation, engaged in what was surely a "council of war". I was so impressed with the orders I got, to deliver my dispatch to him as quickly as possible, as it was urgent and important, that I worked my way up to the door of the Council room, pushed my dispatch under the door, and then knocked loudly, so that those inside could not fail to see it.'

In the hall, O'Donovan found the 'unique and impressive' Countess Markievicz 'very angry with John McNeill' and discovered that the general expectation of the Volunteers and Citizen Army members who had gathered was that the authorities would do precisely what Lord Wimborne wanted to do and crush the incipient rebellion. But the mood was lightened by Thomas MacDonagh. 'I can still recall the laughing face and buoyant step of Tom MacDonagh as he walked to and fro in the hall, with Eamon Bulfin, after the Council meeting finished. His attitude buoyed me up, and gave the impression that things were not so bad as some had been picturing them, just previously, when the opinion was freely expressed that Volunteers, Citizen Army and every Irishman worthy of the name would be arrested before a shot was fired ... We were giving the gods in Dublin Castle credit for having more information and intelligence than they really had.'

Irish Volunteer Marches Cancelled

A SUDDEN ORDER.

The Easter manoeuvres of the Irish Volunteers, which were announced to begin to-day, and which were to have been taken part in by all the branches of the organisation in city and country, were unexpectedly cancelled last night.

The following is the announcement communicated to the Press last evening by the Staff of the Volunteers:—

April 22, 1916.

Owing to the very critical position, all orders given to Irish Volunteers for to-morrow, Easter Sunday, are hereby rescinded, and no parades, marches, or other movements of Irish Volunteers will take place. Each individual Volunteer will obey this order strictly in every particular.

Eoin MacNeill's countermanding order, issued to Irish Volunteers on the eve of the planned Rising. MacNeill believed the rebellion to be doomed, and his order meant that only a small force of Volunteers went into battle on Easter Monday.

HOW EACH SIDE SAW THE GREAT WAR

The outbreak of the First World War seemed at first to put Ireland's internal troubles in the shade. The Home Rule Bill, which was to create an all-Ireland parliament, was suspended until the end of hostilities. The British authorities believed that the war removed the threat of trouble in Ireland. Potential conflict between Ulster Volunteers pledged to fight against Home Rule and the National Volunteers, who had armed themselves to fight for it, seemed to have been defused.

With Ulster Volunteers recruited for the Ulster Division, the Irish Parliamentary Party leader John Redmond matched the offer, and urged members of the Volunteers to serve in the British Army 'wherever the firing line extends'. However, some nationalists wanted to act on the slogan 'England's difficulty is Ireland's opportunity'. A split in the National Volunteers over the war left a smaller faction of Irish Volunteers, which was easier for the militants in the Irish Republican Brotherhood to control.

Their support for the war gradually eroded the authority of John Redmond and his Irish Parliamentary Party as the initial flush of popular enthusiasm turned to wariness about the possibility of forced conscription. The British government feared that disarming the Irish Volunteers

A letter from Eoin MacNeill to a priest, Fr Eugene Nevin, authenticating the countermanding order placed in the Sunday Independent. *MacNeill was aware that regardless of his orders, they might be disobeyed.*

Eamon Bulfin, whom O'Donovan saw with MacDonagh, was a science student who lived at Patrick Pearse's school, St Enda's and who had recently been promoted to the Volunteer headquarters staff as a lieutenant. That morning, he had gone to first Mass at Rathfarnham Church before the intended manoeuvres but, on his way in, read MacNeill's countermanding order in the *Sunday Independent*. After

Mass, as Bulfin was standing outside the church, MacNeill himself approached him and 'asked me to carry a dispatch. I immediately came to the conclusion that this dispatch was a part of the calling off of the manoeuvres and I refused to take it.' Instead he went back to St Enda's and waited 'on tenterhooks' for some word. When none arrived, he went into Liberty Hall, where he was eventually ordered to 'go back to St Enda's and stand-to more or less in readiness for further orders.'

Robert Holland, who was in the 4th Battalion of the Dublin brigade of the Volunteers, had held a meeting with his father and his three brothers on Saturday night. They had received the order to mobilise the next day and they understood it to mean that the Rising was going to happen. His eldest brother, Frank, proposed that the three brothers should go, but that their father should stay. 'He pointed out that my mother was a cripple and we had a young sister then about seven years of age. My father kicked up a row about this decision and said he had spent all his life both in the Fenians and the IRB and that he would go out whether we went out or not.'

At 6am on Sunday, Holland's commander, Con Colbert, called to his house and told him that 'the mobilisation was off pro-tem but I was to mobilise all the men, telling them to stay in their own homes'. Holland spent the rest of the day, until the early evening, passing on Colbert's instructions to the rest of the battalion. He himself was unsure about what was to happen. 'I knew by Sunday morning's paper that the general mobilisation was cancelled but a number of us were in doubt about it being permanent as we expected that a leakage of our intentions would get out and the press would be against us.'

In the evening, Holland went to a céilí at the Donore Avenue branch of the Gaelic League. He left at 10.30pm, went home and went to bed, still unsure what the morning would bring.

Oscar Traynor, an officer in the 2nd Battalion of the Volunteers, had met his commandant, Thomas MacDonagh, and fellow officers on

and Irish Citizen Army in this unsettled atmosphere might create a backlash that would affect army recruitment.

In 1916 some 146,000 Irish were fighting in the Great War. On the Thursday, the 16th (Irish) Division of the British Army lost over 550 men in a single gas attack at Hulluch, Belgium. The crowds of angry women who gathered throughout Easter Week to denounce the rebels were mostly the wives of these soldiers, or widows of those killed.

While many nationalists were among those fighting in the British Army, there was little support for the Easter Rising, and many felt betrayed by it. As news came through to the Front, German soldiers taunted Irish with the message that 'English guns are firing at your wives and children'.

With the change in public attitude following the executions of its leaders, dissatisfaction with the war grew in Ireland. The Nationalist MP and poet, Thomas Kettle, who was killed in the Great War, had prophesised that the Easter rebels 'will go down to history as heroes and martyrs, and I will go down – if I go down at all – as a bloody British officer.'

In all, between 25,000 – 35,000 Irish-born soldiers died in the First World War. However, many of the soldiers who returned to an increasingly nationalist Ireland received a grudging and sometimes hostile welcome.

WHAT WERE THE FORCES THAT FOUGHT IN EASTER WEEK?

The IRB military council was the real architect of the Rising, although many of the insurgents were unaware of its existence. The Irish Republican Brotherhood was a secret society that grew out of the Fenian movement of the 1850s.

After the failure of the Fenian rebellion in 1867 the IRB continued to pursue the aim of Irish independence by force of arms. The movement operated in tandem with a sister organisation in the United States called Clan na Gael. The IRB was sidelined for decades by the constitutional movement for Home Rule but it began to grow in the early years of the 20th century following the return to Ireland of Tom Clarke.

The opportunity for action emerged in 1913 following the formation of the UVF to resist Home Rule. The Irish Volunteers were formed as a response but the organisation was heavily infiltrated from the beginning by the IRB. A secret military council, made up of leading IRB members, plotted throughout 1915 to manipulate the Irish Volunteers into action.

Founded in November 1913 by Eoin MacNeill, professor of early Irish history at UCD, following an enthusiastic response to his call for nationalists to arm themselves to defend Home Rule. The movement immediately attracted tens of thousands of members. Worried about IRB influence, the leader of the Irish Parliamentary Party, John Redmond, insisted on being allowed to nominate half the members of the ruling committee. When Redmond called on the Volunteers to support the British war effort after the outbreak of the First World War, the Volunteers split, with 170,000 men siding with Redmond. Fewer than 10,000 men stayed with MacNeill and his Irish Volunteers. Later there was a division between MacNeill, who thought that a rising should only be attempted if it had a clear chance of success, and the IRB element, which believed it was justified as a means of provoking British repression and radicalising the population.

The vast majority of Volunteers supported John Redmond in 1914, constituting themselves as the National Volunteers. The organisation had declined by 1916 as most of its leading members joined the army at Redmond's instigation. Many of them were fighting for the Allies on the western front when their former comrades staged the Rising in Dublin. In parts of the country the National Volunteers mobilised to help the police restore order until the military arrived on the scene.

THE IRISH CITIZEN ARMY

Founded by James Larkin in 1913 after the bitter Dublin lockout, the Citizen Army was originally intended as a means of protecting strikers against attack. Under the influence of James Connolly, who led the movement after the departure of Larkin to the United Sates in 1914, the Citizen Army took a more militantly nationalist line. As the only military force to accept women members, it attracted a number of radical women political activists to its ranks, the most prominent being Countess Markievicz. A small force of never more than 300, just about 200 of its members gathered at Liberty Hall to join Connolly in rebellion on Easter Monday.

THE ROYAL IRISH CONSTABULARY

Created in 1836, with the 'Royal' title added in 1867, the RIC was an armed police force subject to military drill and discipline. It was deployed throughout the country, apart from in Dublin city, which had its own police. By 1916 the 9,000-strong RIC rarely acted as a paramilitary force and its main functions were to impose public order and engage in normal police duties. The bulk of its members were Irish Catholics, most of them of nationalist political views. A family tradition in policing was a strong factor in recruitment. This is reflected in the fact that five commissioners of the Garda Síochána have been sons or grandsons of RIC men. From February 1916 the RIC had been warning Dublin Castle that a rising was being planned with German support. These reports were ignored.

THE DUBLIN METROPOLITAN POLICE

The DMP was an unarmed police force 1,100 strong, founded in 1836. Mainly concerned with ordinary crime, the DMP also had a G Division, which played an important role in investigating political crime. The force became unpopular in 1913 for the manner in which it brutally broke up workers' gatherings during the lockout. The first casualty of the Rising was DMP policeman Constable James O'Brien, who was shot at the entrance to Dublin Castle on Easter Monday morning. The force was withdrawn from the streets later in the day as unarmed policemen could offer no defence against armed rebels.

THE TRINITY OFFICER TRAINING CORPS

Staff and students of Trinity College who were members of the army reserve. As soon as word reached Trinity on Easter Monday that the Rising was underway, the porters locked the front gate and fastened all the ground-floor windows of the college. At the start the OTC numbered only eight but they immediately opened fire on rebel positions on O'Connell Street. By late afternoon other members of the OTC and some off-duty soldiers had slipped into the grounds. The following day the growing garrison installed machine guns on the parapet and snipers on the roof. From these positions they poured fire on the rebels and severed communications between the GPO and the positions at St Stephen's Green. The action of the OTC was credited with preserving a swathe of the south inner city – Grafton Street, Nassau Street, College Green, Dame Street and Westmoreland Street and D'Olier Street – from destruction.

Easter Saturday. MacDonagh, 'without telling us in actual words that we would be getting into action on the morrow, made it clear that we were going out on something very much more important than ... manoeuvres' . MacDonagh asked if he could stay in Traynor's house that evening, and Traynor replied that it would be an honour. Then he suddenly remembered something. 'I said to him, "By the way, while I would be delighted to have you in our house, I should mention that our next-door neighbour is a policeman." MacDonagh immediately said, "That finishes that."'

Later that evening, Traynor discussed the situation with his captain, Frank Henderson, who told him that there would be a full-scale insurrection the next day but that 'there is a split, that our headquarters staff are divided on the question ... and it may be necessary to arrest some members of the staff'. 'I said that that was an extraordinary state of affairs, and asked him if he knew what Pearse's attitude was. He told me that Pearse was strongly in favour of the insurrection. I said: "That's good enough for me."'

In the morning, Traynor and his close friend Robert Gilligan went to Gilligan's home to collect his military equipment. On their way, they bought a *Sunday Independent* and 'were astonished to find what appeared to be a countermanding order for the Easter manoeuvre. Gilligan said to me "What does this mean? Does it mean that we are divided again?"' The men carried on nonetheless to Father Matthew Park in Fairview, which was being used as an assembly point for the north side of Dublin. They found 'a state bordering on chaos there. Volunteers were coming and going, and there seemed to be doubt in the minds of most of us as to what was to be done.' Eventually, it was agreed that the men would go home but be ready to mobilise again the next day. The large quantities of arms and explosives that had been brought to the park were left overnight, under guard in a pavilion.

Similar scenes were unfolding across the country. The instructions which had reached the would-be rebel leader in Co. Clare, Michael Brennan, were 'so vague as to be incomprehensible'. The county's Volunteers were to supplement their meagre store of arms (four rifles, two revolvers and 30 shotguns) from Casement's shipment, and, if this failed, to raid police barracks for guns. They were then to cut the main roads leading from Clare to Limerick. 'I couldn't even learn in which direction I was supposed to face – whether I was to prevent people getting in [to Limerick] or getting out.' Brennan nevertheless mobilised his men, who waited in the rain for further orders until they were eventually told by the

WEAPONS

The rebels used a mix of weapons, some more effective than others. These included German Mauser rifles and pistols which had been landed at Howth, Co. Dublin, and Kilcoole, Co. Wicklow in 1914, British and Italian rifles, single and double-barrelled shotguns and a small number of revolvers.

The German guns were especially antiquated and dangerous. Many rebels had never held or fired one before. Some describe being knocked across the room or even knocked unconscious by the recoil. These rifles also caused terrible injuries to their targets, which has been cited as one of the reasons why the rebels were so unpopular in the immediate aftermath.

Hand-made grenades were fashioned but proved to be unreliable, with many of them failing to explode.

The rebels also began the Rising with an assortment of other weapons, such as pickaxes, knives, crowbars, sledgehammers and clubs. Some even used pikes, just as had the rebels in 1798. They were not alone. When news of the Rising reached Trinity College, its chief steward passed out pikes confiscated during the 1867 Fenian Rising.

Lord Wimborne, Lord Lieutenant of Ireland from 1915 to 1918, inspects troops outside Dublin Castle in 1916. Originally in favour of arresting militants before the Rising, he agreed to hold off until Easter Monday.

FOOD SHORTAGES THROUGHOUT THE CITY

During the week of the Easter Rising, food shortages became a major problem in the city. Bread was in short supply, especially with Boland's mill in the hands of the rebels. However, the bakery of Johnston Mooney & O'Brien was still operating, and according to *The Irish Times*, 'persons were supplied with only two loaves each, at the ordinary price, and there was a good deal of humour in the spectacle of staid and important professional men walking home with loaves in their arms. At times there was a good deal of mischievous crushing at the bakery door, and some persons suffered from it.'

Some faced the problem of how to pay for the food, according to the report. 'Poor persons naturally suffered most from the food shortage, having received no wages, but others were placed in difficulty by the inability to obtain money from the banks.'

Limerick Provisional Committee of the Volunteers that the Rising was off. Brennan went to Galway to try to contact the local leader, Liam Mellows, but failed to find him. He then tried to enter Limerick but was arrested.

In Co. Cork, more than 1,000 men assembled at various points across the county on Easter Sunday, most hanging around in pouring rain until the early evening and then disbanding.

Denis Lyons, captain of the Volunteers in Kanturk, received orders for Easter Sunday 'to the effect that we were to march to Barley Hill, Newmarket, and with all arms and equipment and three day's rations.' All seven members of his company mobilised, with their one weapon, a .38 revolver and small quantity of ammunition. They marched to Barley Hill, followed by a detective inspector, a sergeant and a constable from the RIC, and joined other local companies, making a total turnout of around 80 volunteers. 'We had no information as to what the purpose of the parade was.' They waited around until five o'clock and then dispersed. Next morning, Lyons and his brother went to Cork city 'in an endeavour to get some information or orders', but the Volunteer leadership was unable to tell them anything. As events unfolded, the Cork leadership would remain paralysed by confusion, indecision and a distrust of Dubliners, especially the Citizen Army. Mary MacSwiney, sister of the Cork republican leader Terence, reported that Dublin had 'made a criminal mistake' and asked: 'Is a fine body of men like the Irish Volunteers to be dragged at the tail of a rabble like the Citizen Army?'

Áine Ceannt, wife of Eamonn Ceannt, had gone to bed at midnight on Easter Saturday night, having two hours earlier seen her husband off to prepare for the Rising. At half past two on Easter Sunday morning, Ceannt arrived back, carrying all his military equipment. 'I was astounded, but he merely remarked, "MacNeill has ruined us – he has stopped the Rising."' Ceannt left again. He called to Liberty Hall to talk to Connolly and to the Metropole Hotel, where Joseph Plunkett was staying, but both men were asleep and could not be disturbed. He went home again. Áine gave him some hot milk and he lay down on his bed, saying 'If I sleep now I would sleep on dynamite'. But he did sleep. When, at 7am on Sunday, a message came for him from Liberty Hall, Áine Ceannt decided not to wake him. Shortly afterwards, Liam Mellows's wife called on her way to Mass. 'I told her we were in great trouble and to pray hard.'

As the morning wore on, the members of Ceannt's 4th Battalion began to arrive at the house, looking for explanations about the countermanding order. Ceannt had in the meantime woken and gone down to Liberty Hall, so Áine suggested that the men wait for him to return. 'Soon our drawing room was uncomfortably filled and the bicycles were stacked four deep in the front garden. To pass the time they asked Captain Douglas ffrench-Mullen, who was a fine pianist, to play for them, which he did – and amongst the airs he chose was The Dead March.'

That evening, there was a concert at Liberty Hall. Nora Connolly sang a ballad: 'I know where I'm going and I know who's going with me.' It had, as her sister Ina reflected, 'a different message for us than for the large audience that packed the hall.'

While she was singing, Eamonn Ceannt was back home. After he had returned from consultations with the other rebel leaders, Ceannt retired to the front room to fill out forms. When his wife asked if she could help, he gave her a bundle of papers to fill up. They were mobilisation orders, commanding his company to assemble again on Easter Monday. The decision had been taken, in spite of the setbacks of the previous days, to go ahead with the rebellion.

REBELS FAIL TO TAKE DUBLIN CASTLE

Monday, April 24th

- ◉ MANOEUVRES BY THE IRISH VOLUNTEERS.

- ◉ THE REBELS TURN OUT IN REDUCED NUMBERS IN DUBLIN.

- ◉ THE REBELS BEGIN OPERATIONS AT NOON, SEIZING THE GENERAL POST OFFICE, BOLAND'S MILL, THE SOUTH DUBLIN UNION, JACOB'S FACTORY AND OTHER BUILDINGS.

- ◉ THE REBELS FAIL TO CAPTURE THE LARGELY UNDEFENDED CENTRE OF THE ADMINISTRATION AT DUBLIN CASTLE BUT OCCUPY THE ADJACENT CITY HALL INSTEAD.

- ◉ PATRICK PEARSE READS THE PROCLAMATION OF THE IRISH REPUBLIC OUTSIDE THE GPO.

- ◉ TRANSPORT AND DISTRIBUTION SERVICES BREAK DOWN THROUGHOUT THE CITY. LARGE SCALE LOOTING BEGINS IN THE O'CONNELL STREET AREA.

- ◉ DURING THE NIGHT, GOVERNMENT TROOPS QUIETLY OCCUPY THE SHELBOURNE HOTEL, OCCUPYING A COMMANDING POSITION OVERLOOKING THE CITIZEN ARMY POSITIONS IN ST STEPHEN'S GREEN.

- ◉ THERE ARE GERMAN ZEPPELIN RAIDS ON THE COASTS OF NORFOLK AND SUFFOLK AND AN AEROPLANE ATTACK ON DOVER.

It was a lovely day for an outing. Ernest Jordison, managing director of the British Petroleum Company in Ireland had hired 'the best motor car in Dublin' to take his friends to Fairyhouse for the Irish Grand National. They met on O'Connell Street and drove up to Dame Street to collect the picnic they would eat at the racecourse. As they drove along, they passed several tram cars full of armed insurgents. They left the city at noon and by the time they arrived at Fairyhouse, there was 'great commotion in the reserved grandstand' and 'rumours of terrible happenings at Dublin'.

The races were on many people's minds. Con O'Donovan, when he went out in the morning to mobilise members of his section of the Volunteers, found different reactions. 'I

A painting depicting the leaders of the rebellion. Patrick Pearse is third from left, Thomas Clarke in the centre and James Connolly second from the right.

can never forget the way in which the news was received in different houses. But what disappointed me most was the number of Volunteers on my list that I found had gone off to Fairyhouse races.' The attendance seems to have included even some prominent IRB men like Harry Boland, the 2nd Battalion quartermaster James Byrne and Seán Boylan, who was meant to have a prominent role in a rising in Meath. At the track, these would-be rebels mingled with many British officers who had also left the city for a day out at the races.

SUNDAY
23

MONDAY
24

TUESDAY
25

WEDNESDAY
26

THURSDAY
27

FRIDAY
28

SATURDAY
29

Arthur Hamilton Norway, head of the Irish Post Office, being a diligent public servant, had letters to write, even though it was a bank holiday. While his wife sat sewing in the Royal Hibernian Hotel on Dawson Street, where the family lived, and their son Nevil went for a ride on his motorbike, he dropped in to his office at the GPO to collect some papers. He was just sitting down at his desk when the phone rang and Sir Matthew Nathan, under-secretary of the Irish administration, asked him to go immediately to Dublin Castle.

'I saw nothing unusual as I walked up to the Castle. Nathan had with him Major Price, the army intelligence officer. He turned to me as I came in and told me there was serious trouble in Kerry, where a ship had been seized with German officers on board, and material for a rising … The position was serious, and he desired me to take immediate steps for denying the use of the Telephone and Telegraph service over large areas of southern Ireland to all but military and naval use … I was just finishing the necessary order, when a volley of musketry crashed out beneath the window. I looked up. "What's that?" I asked. "Oh that's probably the long promised attack on the Castle," cried Nathan, jumping up and leaving the room, while Major Price shouted from the window to some person below, after which he too ran off. I waited for a few minutes, and then went downstairs in search of some explanation. At the foot of the staircase I found all of the messengers huddled together in a frightened crowd. They had seen the policeman at the gate shot through the heart. They were badly shaken.'

Shortly before Arthur Norway had left his family in the Royal Hibernian, Helena Molony had left Liberty Hall with nine other women, all members of the Citizen Army. She was dressed in an Irish tweed costume with a Sam Browne belt slung across it. In it was a revolver. She and the other women had been given the guns that morning by James Connolly, who told them: 'Don't use them except in the last resort.'

Around 11.50am, the women followed a detachment of Citizen Army men, under the command of the Abbey actor Seán Connolly, up Dame Street and then turned left and marched up to the front gate of the Castle. 'Just then', she recalled, 'a police sergeant came out … He thought it was a parade and that it would be going up Ship Street. When Connolly went to go past him, the Sergeant put out his arm and Connolly shot him dead.' The first casualty was not in fact a sergeant but an unarmed constable, 45-year-old James O'Brien.

HOW THE REBEL FORCES WERE DEPLOYED IN DUBLIN

As well as the GPO, City Hall, and St Stephen's Green, the rebels sought to establish strongholds in key areas of the city which would allow them to control or cut off communications with the rest of the country. Their diminished numbers and gaps in their planning, however, meant that their success was patchy. The 1st Battalion occupied the Four Courts and a range of buildings on North King Street and Church Street, and moved as far north as St Peter's Church in Phibsborough, but did not attempt to occupy the strategically important Broadstone Station. The Four Courts garrison saw action early on Monday afternoon, when it fired on a detachment of Lancers escorting ammunition trucks on their way to the Magazine Fort in Phoenix Park. One small section of the battalion moved across the river and occupied the Mendicity Institute near Queen's Street Bridge.

Eamonn Ceannt's 4th Battalion mobilised at Emerald Square, just north of Dolphin's Barn and moved off down Cork Street to occupy Jameson's distillery on Marrowbone Lane and the straggling group of buildings at the South Dublin Union, west of the Guinness Brewery. The SDU was the country's biggest poorhouse, housing 3,000 destitute people. Robert Holland, who ended up in the distillery, found it occupied by 'more women than men' – many of them from the Donore Avenue branch of the Gaelic League, whose céilí he had attended the night before.

The 3rd Battalion, led by Éamon de Valera, had its headquarters in Boland's mill and bakery on Grand Canal Street, to the south-east of the city. Its strategic ambitions were to control the railway lines to the south, to 'dominate' Beggar's Bush Barracks, and to occupy the vital harbour at Kingstown (Dún Laoghaire). A lack of numbers (exacerbated by de Valera's refusal, uniquely among the rebel commandants, to have women in his ranks) meant, however, that the only significant outposts were at Westland Row Station and a small detachment at Mount Street Bridge.

Thomas MacDonagh's 2nd Battalion, of which Oscar Traynor was part, had intended to occupy Amiens Street station, thus preventing the arrival of troop reinforcements by train from Belfast. In the confusion, however, part of the battalion spent most of Monday and Tuesday moving between Fairview and Parnell Square. The main body moved down to St Stephen's Green, and then on to occupy Jacob's factory on Bishop Street. Along the way, it acquired a new vice-commandant, John MacBride, leader of the Irish Brigade in the Boer War, who turned up in a fine blue suit and white spats, bearing nothing more lethal than a malacca cane. A small 10-man unit of the Citizen Army occupied Davy's pub on the northern end of Portobello Bridge to block the movement of troops from Portobello Barracks. It came under heavy attack early on Monday afternoon and was forced to withdraw.

Connolly, who 'was excited because he had shot the policeman dead', shouted to his detachment, 'Get in, get in.' But the rebels, who seemed to Helena Molony unsure of what they were doing, hesitated. 'In a flash, the gates were closed. The sentry went into his box, and began firing.' The rebels withdrew into the adjacent City Hall. The first military action of the Rising had failed in its objective of capturing the Castle.

While this was happening, a group of men was playing football near the Magazine Fort in Phoenix Park. One them, Thomas Leahy, remembered 'playing about with a football for some time to put the sentry then passing the top of the wall off his guard. We then sat down in a group and each man got his instructions and, if successful, to report at the GPO, O'Connell Street, which at the time we did not know was to be our headquarters.' The instructions were: 'The guards were to be disarmed, their arms taken, and tied up in the guardroom. Personnel were to be attacked, the keys or arms and

Dr Edmund McWeeney reads the Proclamation after it was published in Dublin. His son Paul was later a sports editor at The Irish Times.

ammunition stores taken; some of the arms and ammunition were to be destroyed, and as many of the arms as could be taken by us were to be collected by motor car.' Leahy and his comrades said a decade of the Rosary and 'shook hands in case we should never meet again through capture or death'. While one of them distracted the sentry by enquiring about the location of a football pitch, the others rushed in to the guardroom and disarmed the soldiers there. They carried out their orders, soaked the remaining stores with paraffin and set them alight. As they evacuated Mrs Playfair, the wife of the fort's commandant (who was fighting

In all, perhaps 2,000 rebels took part in the Rising. These men were among about 150 that took control of the GPO, which became the rebels' general headquarters during Easter week. From left they are Des O'Reilly, T. Nolan, P. Byrne, Jack Doyle, Tom McGrath, Hugh Thornton, P. Twamley, and an unidentified rebel.

in France), her daughter and her two sons, the eldest boy ran to a house a hundred yards from the fort where there was a telephone. Just as the door was opened, a Volunteer on a bicycle caught up with the boy and shot him three times. He died next morning.

Thomas Leahy got on his bike and 'made for the Liffey gate on the Lucan road side and there found a crowd of people discussing the noise of arms exploding at the Fort and wondering at the cause.' He pretended that 'I had been cycling along from Lucan and stopped where I had seen them, hoping they might have been able to give me some more news.'

Because he had recently returned to Dublin from Barrow-in-Furness, where he worked in a munitions factory, and was wearing a British war service medal, 'they took me to be on holiday and I passed on my way to the city.' Cycling back to the GPO, he came around the top of Dame Street. 'I heard shots and firearms and sought cover by dismounting once again from the bike. It was an attack on the Castle by Citizen Army men, who seemed to be doing well.'

Eamon Bulfin, a lieutenant in the Irish Volunteers, heard the firing from Dublin Castle as he and about 20 men got off a tram from Rathfarnham. He had been in bed at 9am when an order arrived, written in blue pencil by Patrick Pearse's brother, Willie, instructing him to assemble the Rathfarnham company and proceed to Liberty Hall. He got the men on the tram but it stopped at the corner of Dame Street and George's Street because of the firing at the Castle. 'The tram driver and conductor simply abandoned ship and fled. Our party marched down to Liberty Hall … and found no one there.' A messenger arrived with an order to head for the GPO. They loaded their ammunition and supplies on a hand cart and turned up Abbey Street.

Arthur Norway had just left the GPO for Dublin Castle at around 11.50am when a frail, bespectacled man and another man with a bad limp and a walking stick made their

'BOYS WORE SILK HATS PERCHED ON THEIR NOSES OR BACKWARDS AT A DRUNKEN ANGLE ...'

In *On Another Man's Wound*, Ernie O'Malley describes the looting on O'Connell Street on Monday evening: 'I heard the noise of firing; random shots in the distance. People from the slums ... had looted some of the shops. Boys walked around with a bright yellow shoe on one foot, the other bare; women carried apronsful of footwear, stopping at intervals to sit on the curb and try on a pair of satin shoes; then, dissatisfied, fling them away and fit on another and different variety.

'Boys wore silk hats perched on their noses or backwards at a drunken angle. Three of them have cut slits in their hats and placed them over their faces. Water pistols in hands, they were Kelly the Bush Ranger and his gang, with their bullet-proof, bucket helmets.

'Pickets from the GPO fired at the looters, but they fired in the air. Clery's store, a large one, was like an ant heap. Men, women and children swarmed about, carrying off furniture, silks, satins; pushing baby carriages filled with sheets, stockings, garters, curtains.

'Trails, winding and twisting, showed what they had discarded. Pickets were strengthened, looters were fired on, the shots were lower. The looters dropped their armful and scampered away, cursing the armed men. "You dirty bowsies, wait till the Tommies bate your bloody heads off."'

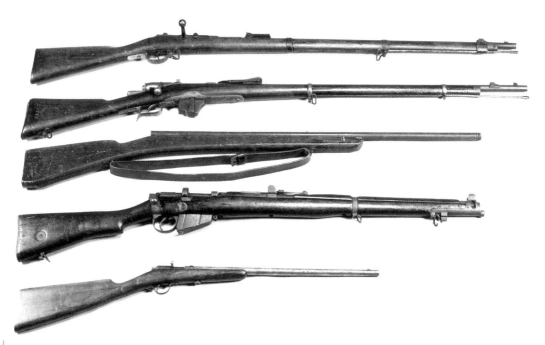

A selection of firearms used during the Rising. The rebels used German Mauser rifles and pistols landed at Howth, Co. Dublin, and Kilcoole, Co. Wicklow in 1914, British and Italian rifles, single and double-barrelled shotguns and a small number of revolvers. However, they also went to battle with pickaxes, knives, crowbars, sledgehammers, clubs and pikes.

painstaking way into O'Connell Street. Tom Clarke, whose health had been damaged by 15 years in prison, and Seán MacDermott, whose leg had been withered by polio, had walked up from Liberty Hall because they were unable to march. They were waiting outside the GPO when about 150 rebels under James Connolly and Patrick Pearse marched up O'Connell Street as far as the Imperial Hotel. Connolly gave a sudden command to wheel left and charge the GPO.

Norway had ensured that a military guard was on duty at the GPO, but the soldiers had no ammunition and could put up no resistance. Once inside, the rebels' immediate task was to persuade baffled customers and staff that they were serious and that bystanders had to leave. When this was done, the rebels sent detachments to the Imperial Hotel, Clery's department store and the shops facing O'Connell Bridge. Pearse, who had been designated as President of the Republic, emerged from the GPO looking 'very pale' and read a proclamation. One sympathetic observer, Stephen McKenna, noted ruefully that 'for once, his magnetism had left him; the response was chilling; a few thin, perfunctory cheers, no direct hostility just then, but no enthusiasm whatever.'

Half an hour later, Eamon Bulfin's detachment arrived at the Prince's Street side of the GPO, just in time to see a company of mounted lancers charge down the street with their sabres drawn. The rebels fired on them from the GPO and the Imperial Hotel, killing four men and scattering the rest. Bulfin 'did not know where the shots were coming from. In the confusion and noise, nobody seemed to give us any attention at all, and the position was looking critical'. He spotted a side window. 'I broke the window with my rifle, and incidentally broke my rifle. Any chaps that were near me, I called them out by name and "hooched" them up the window. Jack Kiely was actually on his hands and knees on the window sill when he was hit by a bullet.'

Once inside, Bulfin reported to Patrick Pearse and was sent to the roof of the building. Up there, he was given the job of hoisting one of two flags. Someone else raised a tricolour. Bulfin was given a green flag with a golden harp and the words 'Irish Republic'. 'The thing I remember most about hoisting it is that I had some kind of hazy idea that the flag should be rolled up in some kind of a ball, so that when it was hauled up, it would break out.' Looking down from the parapet, he saw that people had begun to loot the shops on the street below.

Ernie O'Malley, an 18-year-old medical student, was walking up O'Connell Street and saw two dead horses that had belonged to some of the lancers. 'Seated on a dead horse was a woman, a shawl around her head, untidy wisps of hair straggled across her dirty face. She swayed slowly, drunk, singing: "Boys in khaki, boys in blue, here's the best of jolly good luck to you."'

Robert Holland had been woken at around 7am. He and his brothers Dan and Walter went out around the Inchicore area to mobilise as many Volunteers as they could, and then went to rendezvous at Emerald Square, just north of Dolphin's Barn, at 10 o'clock, where they found Eamonn Ceannt with about a hundred men of his 4th Battalion, including William Cosgrave and Con Colbert. 'There were all makes of rifles and shotguns with revolvers of various types. Some carried swords and bayonets. Some of the men even carried pikes of the crudest kind.' Colbert took Holland's military equipment, gave him a revolver and sent him out on a reconnaissance mission. He was to 'go to the gate of Wellington Barracks and to watch the military' for 'anything suspicious such as troops forming up on

WHO WERE THE MEN WHO SIGNED THE PROCLAMATION?

PATRICK PEARSE

Born in 1879 in Dublin, in Great Brunswick Street – now Pearse Street in his honour. His father, who worked as a church sculptor, was English and his mother was from Co. Meath. Educated first at a private school and then at the Christian Brothers on Westland Row he went on to the Royal University, the forerunner of UCD, where he studied arts and law. He was subsequently called to the bar.

From his school days, Pearse developed a deep interest in the Irish language and he joined the Gaelic League in 1895. He became editor of its paper, *An Claidheamh Soluis*. To advance his ideal of an Ireland 'not free merely but Gaelic as well' he founded a bilingual school, St Enda's, which was first located in Ranelagh and later in Rathfarnham in Dublin. The school was intended as a model for a new education system, with pupils being taught through Irish and with a strong emphasis on nationalism.

He wrote stories, essays and poems in Irish and English and became an exponent of the notion of 'blood sacrifice' in order to redeem the nation's honour.

Initially a supporter of Home Rule, he joined the IRB in 1913 and was co-opted on to its supreme council and elected to the provisional committee of the Volunteers. When the body of the Fenian, Jeremiah O'Donovan Rossa, was brought back from the US in 1915 for burial in Glasnevin Cemetery, Pearse delivered the historic oration that ended with the ringing phrase: 'Ireland unfree shall never be at peace.' In 1916 he was commander-in-chief of the insurgents and regarded as President of the Provisional Republic. After a week's fighting he agreed to surrender unconditionally to prevent the further slaughter of Dublin citizens. He was executed on May 3rd.

SEÁN MACDERMOTT

Born in 1884 in Kiltyclogher, Co. Leitrim, at 16 he emigrated to Glasgow where he worked as a gardener and later as a tram conductor. In 1902 he moved to Belfast, where he worked as a barman. He joined the Celtic League and there met IRB man Bulmer Hobson who asked him to become an organiser for the Dungannon Clubs, set up to promote the IRB in Ulster. In 1906 he joined the Belfast circle of the IRB and was later appointed treasurer of the IRB's supreme council. He became a close friend of Tom Clarke and was appointed manager of the IRB publication *Irish Freedom*.

In 1910 MacDermott became a full-time organiser for Arthur Griffith's Sinn Féin. He spent the next few years travelling the country setting up party branches and organising for the IRB, which was his real mission. He was crippled by an attack of polio in 1912 but he continued his work. Probably the most popular of the senior IRB activists, he was elected to the provisional committee of the Irish Volunteers in 1913 and in 1915 became a member of the military council set up by the IRB to plan the Rising. He fought in the GPO. He was executed on May 12th.

Born in 1878 at Cloughjordan, Co. Tipperary, MacDonagh's parents were teachers. He attended Rockwell College and followed his parents into teaching. He taught in Kilkenny and Fermoy and his interest in the Irish language prompted him to join the Gaelic League. During a trip to the Aran Islands to improve his Irish he met Pearse, and the two became friends. A poet like Pearse, he became the first teacher on the staff of St Enda's. He pursued his studies at UCD, reading for a Master of Arts degree and was appointed to the English department of the university. With Joseph Plunkett he edited the *Irish Review* and helped Edward Martyn to found the Irish

Theatre in 1914. He published several volumes of poetry and his play, *When the Dawn is Come*, was produced at the Abbey Theatre.

When the Irish Volunteers were formed in November 1913 by his UCD colleague Eoin MacNeill, he joined and became director of training the following year. He joined the IRB in 1915 but was only drafted on to the military council a few months before the Rising. He was in command of the Jacob's factory garrison on Bishop Street (now the National Archives) during the Rising. He was executed on May 3rd.

THOMAS MACDONAGH

Born in Dublin in 1887 to a well-off Catholic family, Plunkett's father was a Papal count. He was educated at Belvedere College, Stonyhurst in England and UCD. He suffered from poor health and after graduation from university spent some years in Italy, Egypt and Algeria. On his return to Dublin in 1911 he renewed his friendship with Thomas MacDonagh and with him launched the *Irish Review*. Like MacDonagh and Pearse he was a poet.

He joined the Irish Volunteers in 1913 and his family's house at Kimmage, south of Dublin, was used as a clearing station for arms

imported in 1914. In 1915 Plunkett was inducted into the IRB and he travelled to Berlin to help Roger Casement secure German support for a rising. He then travelled to New York to inform Clan na Gael leaders of the preparations for the revolt. On his return he was appointed to the IRB military council but fell ill in early 1916 and had to undergo throat surgery. Despite his illness, he took his place in the GPO and signed the Proclamation. Like the other signatories he was sentenced to death. He married the artist, Grace Gifford, in his cell in Kilmainham Gaol shortly before his execution on May 4th.

JOSEPH MARY PLUNKETT

THOMAS J. CLARKE

Born in 1857 on the Isle of Wight, the son of a Leitrim-born soldier. The family moved to South Africa but when he was 10 they returned to Dungannon, Co. Tyrone. At 21 he went to the US where he joined Clan na Gael, the American wing of the IRB. In 1883 he was sent to England on a bombing raid, was arrested and sentenced to life. He spent 15 years in jail, much of it in solitary confinement. He returned to Ireland and was made a freeman of Limerick. He married Kathleen, a niece of a prison companion, John Daly.

Unable to get steady work, he returned to the US in 1899. In 1907 he came back to Ireland and opened a tobacconist's shop in what is now Parnell Street. He set about reorganising the IRB and in 1910 published a militantly anti-British journal, *Irish Freedom*. His shop became the centre of republican activity in Dublin and the police saw him as the most dangerous revolutionary in Ireland. By then he was president of the IRB's supreme council. In July 1911, he organised the first pilgrimage to Wolfe Tone's grave in Bodenstown, Co. Kildare, as a counterblast to the visit to Ireland of King George V. In 1915 he became a member of the secret military council established to plot the Rising. When it began he was in the GPO with the other leaders and was asked to be the first to sign the Proclamation. His wife later maintained his leadership of the IRB made him, and not Pearse, the President of the Republic. Clarke was executed on May 3rd.

EAMONN CEANNT

Born in Glenamaddy, Co. Galway in 1881, Eamonn Ceannt moved to Dublin with his family when he was 10 years old. He was educated at the local national school in Glenamaddy and at North Richmond Street CBS in Dublin before going on to UCD. He joined the clerical staff of Dublin Corporation where he was promoted to the position of treasurer of the Corporation. He joined the Gaelic League in 1900 and became passionately involved in the language revival movement. He was also keenly interested in Irish music and played the uileann pipes. He travelled with a group of Irish athletes to Rome for the jubilee of Pope Pius X in 1908 and played a selection of Irish airs on the pipes at the Pope's request.

Ceannt joined Sinn Féin in 1908 and soon afterwards was inducted into the IRB. He was one of the founding members of the Volunteers in 1913. In 1914 he was involved in the Howth gun-running and a year later joined the military council planning the Rising. Many of the council meetings were held in his house in Dublin.

He was placed in command of the detachment that took over the South Dublin Union (now St James's Hospital). He was executed on May 8th.

JAMES CONNOLLY

Born in Edinburgh in 1868 to Irish parents, Connolly started work aged 11 and at 14 joined the British Army. He spent seven years in the army in Ireland and developed an interest in socialism and nationalism. He deserted, returned to Scotland and married a Wicklow woman he had met in Dún Laoghaire. In Edinburgh he worked as a carter, got involved in trade union affairs and became a follower of Karl Marx. He returned to Ireland in 1896 as organiser of the Dublin Socialist Club and founded the *Workers' Republic* newspaper and the Irish Socialist Republican Party. He made a name as a journalist and lecturer, and toured Britain and the US in 1902. He went back to the US in 1903 and spent seven years there. He helped to found the 'Wobblies', the Industrial Workers of the World, a radical US labour organisation.

Connolly returned to Ireland in 1910 and became Ulster organiser for the Irish Transport and General Workers' Union which was led by James Larkin. During the 1913 Dublin lockout, Connolly led when Larkin was sent to prison. The plight of the workers and their families convinced him of the need for action and he founded the Irish Citizen Army. When Larkin went to the US, Connolly became the driving force in the ITGWU. On the outbreak of war he opposed the Allied war effort. He was invited to join the IRB's secret military council and helped plan the Rising. He was a key figure in the GPO and was badly wounded. He was executed on May 12th tied to a chair, as he was unable to stand up.

the square or the filling up of cars with troops.' Holland saw nothing unusual and made his way, as he had been instructed, to Watkins' brewery on Ardee Street, which the battalion was to occupy as an outpost to its main objectives at the South Dublin Union (the country's biggest poorhouse) and the Jameson's distillery at Marrowbone Lane

Holland arrived at the brewery at noon, but found that the gate was locked with 'a very rowdy crowd of women of the poorer class around it. These consisted mainly of British soldiers' wives and their dependants. They were expressing in no uncertain fashion their sympathy with the caretaker of the brewery who they said was manhandled by a lot of Sinn Féiners who had gone in and beaten him up. I knocked on the gate to get in and after about two minutes knocking and kicking at the gate I found I could not get in. I made up my mind to come away.' As he was leaving he met his brother Dan and another Volunteer bringing a hand-cart loaded with arms, ammunition and tinned food and told them 'there was no chance of them of them getting in there.'

Holland made for Marrowbone Lane instead, and as he was walking along Cork Street, he heard 'fairly heavy' rifle fire. 'People started to run in all directions.' When Holland got to Marrowbone Lane, 'about three quarters of the way down in an elbow bend of the road a lot of people had congregated on the bend and a British soldier was lying dead in the centre of the road. The people advised me not to go any further but I said I lived down that way.' Having reached the garrison in the distillery, he was asked to go back and bring the cartload of supplies to them. He did so and eventually got back at around 3pm. He was not unhappy to find that 'there seemed to be more women than men in the garrison' and that most of the 'girls' had been at the céilí he had attended the previous night. He was assigned to a sniper's post on the top floor of the building and given 'some brush handles and some long sticks with about a half dozen caps and hats. I put the caps and hats on the long sticks and put them at the edge of the windows so that they could be seen from outside and with the intention of drawing fire from any British military outside.'

THE WITNESSES

Augustine Birrell was chief secretary for Ireland. A well-known essayist and British cabinet minister, he had been transferred to Ireland in 1907.

Eamon Bulfin attended Patrick Pearse's school, St Enda's, and became a member of the Irish Volunteers and IRB. He was stationed at the GPO during the Rising.

Áine Ceannt was the wife of Eamonn Ceannt, one of the Rising's leaders.

Liam T. Cosgrave joined the Irish Volunteers in 1913, and was present at the landing of the Howth rifles. He served under Eamonn Ceannt at the South Dublin Union during the Rising.

Capt. Arthur Annan Dickson was a Lloyd's Bank employee in Devon at the outbreak of the Great War and gained an army commission in 1916, despite having been previously rejected on medical grounds.

Capt. E. Gerrard was educated at Clongowes College, before receiving an army commission. He served in the Dardanelles, Turkey before being stationed at Athlone in April 1916. On leave in Dublin during the Rising, he was stationed at Beggar's Bush Barracks.

John Joly was an inventor, physicist and Professor of Geology and Mineralogy in Trinity College Dublin, where he was also attached to the army's Officer Training Corps. Born in 1857, he had previously published pioneering work on the age of the earth and developed radiotherapy as a cancer treatment.

Ernest Jordison was managing director of British Petroleum in Ireland.

Arthur Hamilton Norway was secretary of the General Post Office in Ireland, with his office becoming the rebel headquarters during the Rising. His wife, Mary Louisa, was living at the Royal Hibernian Hotel at the time, and wrote several letters during the week.

Robert Holland, from Inchicore, Dublin, attended his first Fianna Éireann meeting aged 12, and got his first gun when the Howth rifles landed. A member of the Volunteers and the IRB, he turned 19 during the Rising. He was stationed at Jameson's distillery, at Marrowbone Lane.

Dick Humphreys was a 20-year-old former pupil of St Enda's. A member of the Volunteers since his school days, he was at the GPO during the Rising.

Around the time Robert Holland had arrived back at the distillery, on the Dundrum Road, in the foothills of the Dublin Mountains, John Joly was out for a walk. Joly was Professor of Geology and Mineralogy at Trinity College Dublin and a scientist of international repute who pioneered, among other things, colour photography, the calculation of the age of the earth and the use of radiation in cancer treatment. He was enjoying 'a day of peaceful thoughts if ever there was one', when around 120 British Army veterans and civilian volunteers passed him by. They were members of an auxiliary force that wore civilian clothes with armbands emblazoned with the letters GR – Georgius Rex – giving rise to the derisive nationalist nicknames 'Gorgeous Wrecks' and 'God's Rejected'. They had been in Ticknock, where they had conducted a sham fight against the GRs of Kingstown and Greystones.

General Sir John Grenfell Maxwell was sent to Ireland late in the week as commander-in-chief of military forces.

Helena Molony was affiliated with Cumann na mBan – the women's arm of the Irish Volunteers – and the Irish Citizen Army. She was involved in the raid on Dublin Castle.

Sir Matthew Nathan had been under-secretary for Ireland since 1914. He was a former governor of Sierra Leone, the Gold Coast and Hong Kong.

Elizabeth O'Farrell was a midwife at the National Maternity Hospital, Holles Street, and member of Cumann na mBan. She acted as a courier both before and during the Rising.

Ernie O'Malley was an 18-year-old medical student and eye-witness to the Rising.

James Stephens was a poet and novelist best-known for both his retelling of Irish fairy tales, and also for works of fiction based on Irish myths. An eye-witness to the Easter Rising, his book, *The Insurrection in Dublin*, was published soon after the event.

Joseph Sweeney, originally from Donegal, was a former St Enda's pupil. At UCD by 1916, he was an Irish Volunteer stationed at the GPO during the Rising.

A noted soccer player for Belfast Celtic in his youth, **Oscar Traynor** was 30 years old at the time of the Rising, when as an Irish Volunteer he saw action at O'Connell Street.

Thomas Walsh, and his brother **James**, were members of the Irish Volunteers positioned first at Boland's mill and then Clanwilliam House, near Mount Street Bridge, during the Rising.

Martin Walton was a member of Fianna Éireann and joined the Irish Volunteers three weeks before the Rising. A 15-year-old at the time, he acted as a courier between the GPO and Jacob's factory.

Lord Wimborne was lord-lieutenant, the king's representative in Ireland. Previously an MP, he had been appointed to Ireland in 1915.

The Irish Volunteers commandeered carts to create a barricade on Dublin's Townsend Street. When an elderly man attempted to free his cart from a barricade on St Stephen's Green, he was shot dead by rebels.

'The GRs came swinging along at a steady pace, their faces towards the city. An officer on horseback led them. As he passed us, we recognised in him Major Harris of the Officer Training Corps of the University of Dublin. He stopped us. "Have you heard that the Sinn Féiners have risen in Dublin, and seized the General Post Office and Stephen's Green, and shot several of the police?" The veterans passed on their way to the city, leaving us bewildered.' An hour later, the GRs, who were either unarmed or had rifles but no ammunition, were fired on by rebels on Haddington Road. Four were killed and nine wounded.

Joly made his way to the college, a key location at the centre of the city, which the rebels, for some unknown reason, had made no attempt to occupy, even though it was defended by little more than the student Officer Training Corps (OTC). When news of the Rising had reached the College a few hours earlier, the Chief Steward Joseph Marshall directed the porters, whom he armed 'with Fenian Pikes, which I had seized whilst in the DMP in 1867', to lock the front gate and to invite into the College all passing soldiers, including some Australians, New Zealanders, Canadians and South Africans. Joly recalled that, 'It happened that Trinity College seemed almost without defenders. Major Tate, the CO, was unfortunately away. But Captain Alton of the OTC, Lieutenant Luce of the Royal Irish Rifles, who was home from the front on sick leave, and Lieutenant Waterhouse were fortunately at hand. A few boys in khaki were about. There was no doubt of the seriousness of the position. Help from military or police was not to be expected for some time – possibly for some days. That the college had not already been captured was most inexplicable. It was obviously the most central and commanding position in the city. There was the additional attraction of the military stores of the OTC depot. In this were kept some hundreds of service rifles and many thousands of rounds of ammunition.'

Helena Molony was sent from the City Hall to the GPO to ask for reinforcements. As she was leaving, one of the rebels approached her 'nearly in tears: "Miss Molony, give that note – it is a note for the ould mott" – his wife'. Walking down Dame Street, she met the left-wing journalist Francis Sheehy Skeffington 'looking very white and dispirited', distressed by the looting. She carried on to the GPO, delivered her message and walked back to City Hall. She was on the roof at around 2pm when she saw a stray bullet hit Seán Connolly. 'He was bleeding very much from the stomach. I said the Act of Contrition into his ear. We had no priest ... His young brother Matt, who was only 15, was also on the roof and saw his brother dying.'

While Connolly was dying, the writer James Stephens was encountering the other main detachment of the Citizen Army, under Michael Mallin, at St Stephen's Green. Mallin's force, with Constance Markievicz as second-in-command, had occupied the Green at noon, in the process shooting dead an unarmed DMP constable, Michael Lahiff from Co. Clare. Lahiff had been shot three times for 'refusing to leave his post'. Stephens was unaware of what was happening until he left his office in the National Gallery to go for lunch and was

ABBEY PLAY CANCELLED

On Easter Monday there was to be a matinee performance in the Abbey Theatre of W.B. Yeats's *Cathleen Ní Houlihan*. The play was co-authored with Augusta Gregory in 1902, and with Maud Gonne as the lead in this parable of Ireland's troubles it became an icon of the country's struggle. The story is set on the day in 1798 that the French landed in support of the United Irishmen, and features a poor old woman convincing a young groom to join the rebellion. When he does so, Cathleen Ní Houlihan is transformed into a young woman 'with the walk of a queen'.

Alongside it was to run a new play, *The Spancel of Death* by TH Nally, based on real events surrounding supposed witchcraft in 18th-century Mayo. Although sold out, it was cancelled because of the Rising and the play wasn't performed until it was revived briefly in the 1980s.

On Easter Monday there was to be a matinee performance in the Abbey Theatre of W.B. Yeats's Cathleen Ní Houlihan. *With Maud Gonne as the lead, the play was a parable of Ireland's struggle for independence.*

walking down Merrion Row when he noticed that people were gathering in a mood of 'silence and expectation and excitement'. He asked what was happening. 'Don't you know? The Sinn Féiners have seized the city this morning.' Stephens ran towards the Green and heard 'rifle fire ... like sharply-cracking whips'. He saw armed men in the park and a rough barricade of carts and motor cars built across the road. He went back to his office and returned to St Stephen's Green at 5pm.

As he watched, Michael Cavanagh approached the barricade. He was an elderly man and was involved in the theatre. His theatrical effects were in a cart – known as a lorry – and it was in the barricade. He started to pull it free when armed men appeared at the park railings,

SUNDAY
23

MONDAY
24

TUESDAY
25

WEDNESDAY
26

THURSDAY
27

FRIDAY
28

SATURDAY
29

Stamps issued by An Post to mark the fiftieth anniversary of the Rising. The series featured the seven signatories of the Proclamation.

shouting 'Put down that lorry. Let out and go away. Let out at once.' He kept pulling until the men fired some warning shots. He walked over to speak to the rebels. '"Go and put back that lorry or you are a dead man. Go before I count four. One, two, three, four ..." A rifle spat at him, and in two undulating movements the man sank on himself and sagged to the ground. I ran to him with some others, while a woman screamed unmeaningly, all on one strident note. The man was picked up and carried to a hospital beside the Arts Club. There was a hole in the top of his head, and one does not know how ugly blood can look until it has been seen clotted in hair. As the poor man was being carried in, a woman plumped to her knees in the road and began not to scream but to screech. At that moment the Volunteers were hated.'

Capt. E. Gerrard, home on leave from the Dardanelles, was walking in civilian clothes along Grafton Street when he too saw the rebels in St Stephen's Green. 'I realised there was something serious on, and I went home and got my uniform.' He went to Beggar's Bush Barracks at around 8pm and found it almost undefended. There were no arms and little ammunition.

FIRST IRISH FILM SHOT IN 1916

In August 1916, *O'Neill of the Glen*, the first film produced by the Film Company of Ireland, was shown in the Bohemian Theatre, Dublin. A cameraman from the Film Company of Ireland photographed audience members as they entered the theatre, and the footage of the patrons was screened at subsequent screenings as a way of enticing repeat business. The film itself is now presumed to be lost. Other films made by the company that year included *Fun at a Finglas Fair*, *Puck Fair Romance* and *Irish Jarvey Tales*.

'There were Sir Frederick Shaw, myself, one or two ranker officers, four non-commissioned officers, and about 10 men, three of whom were invalids.' Just two of them had ever fired a shot in anger – Gerrard during the war; and Shaw, who was now commander of the 2nd battalion of the Royal Irish Fusiliers, against the Fenians in 1867.

Part of the task of Éamon de Valera's 3rd Battalion at Boland's mill was to 'dominate' the barracks, but he did not realise that, as Gerrard put it, 'There was nothing in Beggar's Bush Barracks if only they had rushed it.'

Driving back from Fairyhouse and looking down O'Connell Street from Parnell Square, Ernest Jordison 'actually saw boys with cricket bats and balls, playing in the middle of the road', and two dead horses lying amid huge pools of blood. At Annesley Bridge, he was stopped by a group of rebels. He told them he was coming from the races at Fairyhouse. 'One Volunteer asked me if Civil War had won [the Grand National]. I told him it was third.'

At around 5pm, Robert Holland, at his sniper's post, in Marrowbone Lane distillery, fired his first shots in anger. Looking out on a piece of open ground called Fairbrother's Fields, he caught 'my first sight of khaki in the cabbages'. He sent a warning to his fellow rebels, then 'the soldiers appeared to delay and one of them seemed to walk up and down giving them some orders as to what to do. I sighted this particular individual but before I had time to press the trigger of my rifle I was taken by surprise myself. A volley of shots rang out both from over and under me and then I fired. The soldiers went down and returned the fire. This fire kept on until dark.'

As evening fell, it began to rain. During the night, government troops slipped into the Shelbourne Hotel, unnoticed by the rebels and therefore unopposed, giving themselves a commanding position overlooking St Stephen's Green. James Stephens lay awake in his flat on the Green. 'Every five minutes a rifle cracked somewhere, but about a quarter to twelve sharp volleying came from the direction of Portobello Bridge, and died away after some time ... In another quarter of an hour there were volleys from Stephen's Green direction, and this continued with intensity for about 25 minutes. Then it fell into a sputter of fire and ceased. I went to bed about four o'clock convinced that the Green had been rushed by the military and captured, and that the Rising was at an end.'

A BAPTISM OF FIRE

Tuesday, April 25th

- GOVERNMENT FORCES ARRIVE IN THE CITY BY TRAIN OVERNIGHT FROM BELFAST AND THE CURRAGH.

- MACHINE GUN FIRE FROM THE ROOF OF THE SHELBOURNE HOTEL FORCES THE REBELS TO LEAVE THEIR POSITIONS IN ST STEPHEN'S GREEN AND WITHDRAW INTO THE COLLEGE OF SURGEONS.

- GOVERNMENT TROOPS RETAKE CITY HALL AND THE NEARBY OFFICES OF THE DAILY EXPRESS.

- THE DERANGED CAPTAIN BOWEN-COLTHURST ARRESTS THREE INNOCENT CIVILIANS, INCLUDING THE PACIFIST FRANCIS SHEEHY SKEFFINGTON, AND HAS THEM SHOT THE NEXT MORNING.

- LORD WIMBORNE DECLARES MARTIAL LAW.

- ZEPPELINS RAID KENT AND ESSEX, AND GERMAN SHIPS BOMBARD LOWESTOFT AND GREAT YARMOUTH. THE BRITISH ASSUME (WRONGLY) THAT THESE ATTACKS ARE BEING MADE IN SUPPORT OF THE IRISH REBELS.

Before dawn, three young men on bicycles reached the foot of Grafton Street and were cycling past the Provost's house in Trinity College. They were armed rebel dispatch riders, bringing messages from Stephen's Green to the GPO. The colonial troops who were defending the college opened fire and killed 20-year-old Gerald Keogh. According to John Joly: 'It was wonderful shooting ... Four shots were fired. Three found their mark in the head of the unfortunate victim. Another of the riders was wounded and escaped on foot. The third abandoned his bicycle and also escaped. This shooting was done by the uncertain light of the electric lamps, and at a high angle downwards from a lofty building. The body was brought in.

'Later I saw him. In no irreverent spirit I lifted the face-cloth. He looked quite young; one might almost call him a boy. The handsome waxen face was on one side concealed in blood. Poor boy! What crime was his? That of listening to the insane wickedness and folly

MONDAY
24

TUESDAY
25

WEDNESDAY
26

THURSDAY
27

FRIDAY
28

SATURDAY
29

Members of the Irish Citizen Army on the roof of Liberty Hall prior to the Rising.

BROTHERS IN ARMS ON DIFFERENT SIDES

Martin Mullen, a 23-year-old Dublin bricklayer was a day late for the Rising. He had read, and obeyed, Eoin MacNeill's countermanding order in the *Sunday Independent* that had called off the 'manoeuvres' scheduled for Easter Monday. Almost exactly a year earlier his younger brother James, a volunteer in a different uniform, had lost his sight at Gallipoli and at this stage was in hospital in Alexandria.

Martin rose early, and went to the back garden of the family's terraced house near the Coombe. His German Mauser rifle, brought ashore two years earlier at Howth, had been wrapped in an overcoat and buried there in anticipation of future action. Having dug up and cleaned the rifle he headed for Jacob's biscuit factory accompanied by his girlfriend, May McMahon. At the entrance to Bishop Street they became involved in an event that affected them deeply.

They were confronted by a group of 'Ring-Paper Women'. These dependants of British soldiers earned their nickname from their allowance books that contained printed circles to be stamped when payment was made.

The women, screaming abuse at the rebels and spitting at the couple, blocked

preached by those older and who ought to be wiser than he. And was not he, after all, but one of those who carry to its logical conclusion the long crusade against English rule which for generations has kept peace from Irish hearts?'

Another young rebel, Martin Walton, was just 15, though at six feet tall, he looked older. He had been in the Volunteers for just three weeks. When he got up on Tuesday morning, he found that his parents had taken the valves from the tyres in his bicycle to prevent him from going into the city centre to join the rebels. He convinced them, however, that he had to go to work or risk losing his job. When he got to the GPO, he was told to go to Jacob's factory in Wexford Street. He had hardly ever been south of the Liffey and had to ask directions as he went along. 'When I arrived then at Jacob's the place was surrounded by a howling mob roaring at the Volunteers inside, "Come out to France and fight, you lot of so-and-so slackers." And then I started shouting up to the balustrade, "Let me in, let me in." And then I remember the first blood I ever saw shed. There was a big, very, very big tall woman with something very heavy in her hand and she came across and lifted up her hand to make a bang at me. One of the Volunteers upstairs saw this and fired and I just remember seeing her face and head disappear as she went down like a sack. That was my baptism of fire, and I remember my knees nearly going out from under me. I would have sold my mother and father and the Pope just to get out of that bloody place.'

At around the same time, Patrick Pearse, in the GPO, was writing a report for a Republican newsheet to be printed at Liberty Hall: 'The Republican forces everywhere are fighting with splendid gallantry. The populace of Dublin are plainly with the Republic, and the officers and men are everywhere cheered as they march through the streets.' Pearse also issued a 'Manifesto to the Citizens of Dublin': 'The country is rising in answer to Dublin's call and the final achievement of Ireland's freedom is now, with God's help, only a matter of days … Irish

Regiments in the British Army have refused to act against their fellow-countrymen.'

The optimistic pronouncements of the rebel leaders filtered down to the fighters. In Marrowbone Lane distillery, Robert Holland woke up to his nineteenth birthday and started to hear the good news. 'We are holding the whole city. I hear that all the country is marching on Dublin and it is only a matter of a few days until we will have the job done. All we have to do is to keep it up until they arrive'. After a few hours of exchanging fire with troops at the Dolphin's Barn end of the building, he met his 15 year-old brother Walter, who reinforced the buoyant mood: 'He had heard that the Germans had landed in Galway and that the Volunteers from all over the country were on their way to Dublin.'

Overnight, in fact, the military authorities had begun to get to grips with the reality of the rebellion and to mount an organised response. Troops, including Brigadier General W.H.M. Lowe, reached the city by train from Belfast and the Curragh during the night, and by twenty past five in the morning, the whole Curragh Mobile Column of 1,600 men was in Dublin. Shortly afterwards, it was joined by 1,000 men of the 25th Irish Reserve Infantry Brigade. By 4.20pm the number of troops available to the authorities had risen to around 3,000 and more were preparing to sail from Britain.

One of the troops rushed by train to Dublin overnight was 18-year-old Edward Casey a 'Cockney Irish' kid from a poor family of Irish exiles in the East End of London. He had joined the Royal Dublin Fusiliers and had already served at Ypres and Salonika. He arrived in Dublin at daybreak. 'Marching in columns of fours, we were told by our officers "This is not war: it's rebellion." Our Company was detailed to cover the Four Courts ... My post was lying down behind an iron urinal on the banks of the Liffey, and right opposite the Guinness Brewery. Streets were deserted, although on the way from the station, the crowds of men and women greeted us with raised fists and curses. I noticed a

their way. They called on a passing postman to help them stop Martin from joining the rebels. A shot rang out from inside Jacob's. The postman was hit. The women scattered. Martin Mullen joined his comrades but after the surrender and his internment at Frongoch in north Wales, he opted out of political activity. Unlike other family members, he took no part in the War of Independence or the Civil War.

Inside Jacob's, Martin Mullen was surprised to meet a neighbour. Joe Byrne was a soldier attached to an English county regiment who was home on leave from the Front. He had impulsively decided to join the rebels, shed his khaki uniform and gone to Jacob's in civvies. Loyalties were not all that clearly defined at the time.

When the fighting ended (and there was very little fighting at Jacob's), the insurgents created a diversion to smuggle Byrne to safety. Had he been captured he would undoubtedly have faced the firing squad as a deserter.

Martin and James Mullen had been in the IRB and at the Howth gun-running together in 1914. They had attended meetings at Merchant's Quay in Dublin with Liam Mellows, Garry Houlihan and Colm Ó Lochlainn, later of the Three Candles Press. They parted ways when James had a blazing row with his tyrannical father and took an escape route that led to his encounter with a piece of Turkish shrapnel in the Dardanelles.

The Mullen brothers met different fates. Martin married May McMahon and was the father of eight sons. He died in the 1950s, a senior official in Dublin Corporation. James, a civil servant in London, lived until 1979, his sight just partially restored, though he was almost totally deaf. He never married. The love of his life, Marie Butler from Bordeaux, died before their planned wedding.

dead horse and a tram car pushed over on its side ... I was standing behind my iron box when I noticed an old lady walking slowly along the street. When she was in hearing distance, I yelled "Halt! Who goes there?" "Oh Jesus, Mary and Joseph!" came the reply. It was amusing but to me very sad. That old lady with her Irish accent reminded me so much of my mother. Leading her by the arm to the shelter of the urinal, I told her she may have to stay a while. Shots were being fired now and again from the big concrete building across the road.' (Presumably the Mendicity Institute.)

Con O'Donovan, now in the Four Courts garrison, noticed the tension that the first experience of combat exerted on one of his comrades. 'One poor fellow, who was certainly very unfitted for soldiering, even of the mild kind that we were experiencing ... became so unbalanced from the strain that I had to get him down to the ground floor, with a request that he be kept there and not given a rifle again. A sign, hanging outside the gun shop of Keegan and making a peculiar sound as it swayed in the wind, became for him an armoured car on which he wanted to fire, but could not steady himself sufficiently to do so. After that, I got his rifle from him, and manoeuvred him to the kitchen.'

For O'Donovan himself, the pressure came in part from the sporadic nature of the shooting. 'We were really suffering from the strain of looking for a soldier to fire at, and I remember well the callous and, shall I say, brutal pleasure I felt when I "picked off" one who was crossing Grattan Bridge, although he dodged from side to side, and kept his head low most of the time. Another who fell to one of our group was too easy to mark. He walked out of Chancery Street, in full kit. Our man at a loop-hole saw him, and asked me what would he do. Well, what could he do? Here was a soldier, armed and probably looking for a chance to fire on us? One bullet did it, and then the marksman raised his hat, and said, "He's dead, or dying now, anyhow. May the Lord have mercy on his soul."'

"DAILY EXPRESS."
FREE INSURANCE.
£1,000 at death   SEE
£1 10s. a week while disabled   PAGE
£500 for loss of eye or limb   **6.**
And other benefits.

Daily ☙ Express

Late War EDITION

NO. 5,008.   LONDON, WEDNESDAY, APRIL 26, 1916.   ONE HALFPENNY.

FREE ADVERTISEMENTS FOR DISABLED SOLDIERS AND SAILORS.
SEE PAGE SIX

Secret Session—Dublin Revolt—Naval Raid on England.

CRAZY REBELLION IN IRELAND.

ARMED SINN FEINERS SEIZE POST OFFICE AND STREETS IN DUBLIN.

CITY ISOLATED.

11 KILLED AND 17 WOUNDED IN THE FIGHTING.

A grave rebellion in Dublin has followed the attempt by a German vessel to land arms and ammunition in Ireland and the arrest of Sir Roger Casement, the renegade ex-Consul. Official news available last night showed that there were two centres of the rebellion, which was organised by Sinn Feiners, as follows:—

North of the River: The Post Office, Sackville-street, Abbey-street, and the Quays.

South of the River: St. Stephen's Green.

Telegraph and telephone wires had been cut.

Troops from the Curragh have arrived, and have the situation well in hand.

The casualties reported number eleven or twelve killed and seventeen or nineteen wounded, as follows:—

Officers killed, three; wounded, four or five.

Soldiers killed, four or five; wounded, seven or eight.

Policemen killed, two.

Loyal volunteers killed, two; wounded, six.

The casualties among the rebels are not known.

LIMITED TO DUBLIN.

The following official statement was issued last evening by the Chief Secretary for Ireland:—

At noon yesterday serious disturbances broke out in DUBLIN. A large body of men affiliated with the Sinn Feiners, mostly armed, occupied STEPHEN'S GREEN and took possession forcibly of the POST OFFICE, where they cut the telegraphic and telephonic wires. Houses were also occupied in STEPHEN'S GREEN, SACKVILLE STREET, ABBEY STREET, and along the QUAYS.

In the course of the day soldiers arrived from the CURRAGH, and the situation is now well in hand.

So far as it known here—

Three military officers, four or five soldiers, two loyal volunteers, and two policemen have been killed, and

Four or five military officers, seven or eight soldiers, and six loyal volunteers wounded.

No exact information has been received of casualties on the side of the Sinn Feiners.

Reports received from CORK, LIMERICK, ENNIS, TRALEE, and both Ridings of TIPPERARY show that no disturbances of any kind have occurred in those localities.

QUESTIONS IN PARLIAMENT.

The first news of the rebellion was announced in the House of Commons yesterday by Mr. Birrell, in reply to a question by Colonel James Craig (U., Down, E.), who asked if the Chief Secretary for Ireland was prepared to make a statement regarding the situation in the Irish capital.

Mr. Birrell said:—

At noon yesterday grave disturbances broke out in Dublin. The Post Office was forcibly taken possession of, and telegraphic communication was cut off. In the

STREET MAP OF DUBLIN.

DOWNING STREET CONFERENCE.

Mr. Asquith returned to Downing-street early yesterday morning, and invited the Cabinet to meet him later, while Sir E. Carson, Secretary for Ireland, also arrived shortly after daybreak, accompanied by Mr. Samuel, the Home Secretary.

EAGER FOR WAR.

GERMAN NEWSPAPERS WANT A BREAK WITH THE U.S.

SIR R. CASEMENT'S TRIAL.

BROUGHT TO LONDON IN MILITARY CUSTODY.

HIS ACTS IN GERMANY.

The following official statement in connection with the arrival of Sir Roger Casement was issued yesterday:—

Sir Roger Casement, whose arrest in connection with the abortive attempt to land arms in Ireland from a German vessel was announced yesterday, was brought to London on Sunday morning.

He was met at Easton by officers from Scotland-yard, and is now detained in military custody.

It is understood that evidence as to his proceedings in Germany since the outbreak of war will be printed at an early date.

In the House of Commons yesterday Mr. Pemberton Billing put the following question to the Prime Minister:—

"Is it a fact that Sir Roger Casement has been brought to London, and can the Prime Minister give the House and the nation an assurance that this traitor will be shot forthwith?" (Loud laughter and cheers.)

Mr. Asquith replied: "I do not think that is a question that ought to be put to me at present." (Cheers.)

The law of high treason and its penalties are explained on Page 4.

IRELAND'S RULERS.

The head of the Executive Government of Ireland at Dublin Castle is Lord Wimborne, who succeeded the Earl of Aberdeen as Lord Lieutenant last year. He is in his forty-fourth year, and fought with the Yeomanry in South Africa.

Under the Lord Lieutenant the most important official at Dublin Castle is Under-Colonel Sir Matthew Nathan, who became Permanent Under-Secretary in October last, in succession to Sir James Dougherty.

He is fifty-four years of age and has had a distinguished career both in the military and colonial services.

OFFICIAL REPORT.

THE SECRET SESSION.

CABINET PLANS TO SECURE 200,000 MORE MEN.

AID FOR THE MARRIED

GRANTS TO BE MADE UP TO £104 A YEAR.

Parliament sat in secret yesterday, and both Houses were informed of the Government's recruiting proposals and plans for the financial relief of married men called to the colours. The secret session will be continued to-day.

Compulsion for all is to be enforced unless:—

50,000 unattached men are recruited before May 27.

15,000 a week are obtained after that date.

200,000 are obtained in all.

NOT ENOUGH MEN.

AIR ATTACKS BY THE BRITISH.

ENEMY AERODROME IN BELGIUM BOMBED.

GOOD RESULTS.

ADMIRALTY, Wednesday, 12.15 a.m.

On the morning of the 23rd inst., in spite of most inclement weather a British air attack was carried out by naval aeroplanes upon the enemy aerodrome at Mariakerke.

29 COMBATS IN THE AIR

British Official.

FROM SIR DOUGLAS HAIG.
GENERAL HEADQUARTERS,
Tuesday, 10.15 p.m.

LIQUID FIRE ATTACK.

FRESH GERMAN FAILURE AT THE DEAD MAN.

French Official.
PARIS, Tuesday, April 25.

COMBINED NAVAL AND AIR RAID.

LOWESTOFT BOMBARDED BY GERMAN BATTLE-CRUISERS.

ENEMY'S FLIGHT AFTER ACTION WITH LIGHT SQUADRON.

THE NAVAL RAID.

About 4.30 this morning the German battle cruiser squadron, accompanied by light cruisers and destroyers, appeared off Lowestoft. The local naval forces engaged it, and in about twenty minutes it returned to Germany chased by our light cruisers and destroyers.

On shore two men, one woman, and a child were killed. The material damage seems to have been magnificent.

So far as is known at present two British light cruisers and a destroyer were hit, but none was sunk.

SEAPLANES ATTACK SUBMARINES.

THE AIR RAID.

WAR OFFICE, Tuesday, 9 p.m.

AIR AND SEA RAID ON ZEEBRUGGE.

GERMAN DESTROYERS HIT AND DRIVEN INTO PORT.

FOURTEEN BOMBS ON ONE TOWN.

LONDON STOCKBROKER INJURED.

The Rising as it was reported in British newspaper, The Daily Express. *Its headlines read: 'Secret Session – Dublin Revolt … Crazy Rebellion in Ireland.' It also reports on a naval raid on England by German battle-cruisers.*

Francis Sheehy Skeffington, on the right, would become one of the tragic figures of the 1916 Rising. A journalist and pacifist, while attempting to organise a group to stop the looting, he was arrested and executed. Here, he is pictured with Irish Volunteer, James White, in 1913.

Hanna Sheehy Skeffington, wife of the murdered Francis Sheehy Skeffington.

THE MORNING A MAD CAPTAIN ORDERED THE DEATH OF A PACIFIST AND TWO JOURNALISTS

At around 8pm on Tuesday evening, Francis Sheehy Skeffington was walking from the city centre towards his home in Rathmines. His efforts to organise a civic body to prevent looting had attracted both admirers and detractors, and as he approached Portobello Bridge a crowd followed him, some of its members calling his name. A young officer of the Royal Irish Rifles at a checkpoint on Portobello Bridge assumed that Skeffington was causing trouble and had him detained and sent to Portobello barracks. Under interrogation, he pointed out that he was against militarism and in favour of passive resistance.

At about 11.10pm, Capt. J.C. Bowen-Colthurst, a veteran of the Battle of Mons who had been invalided home, led a raid on the Camden Street home and tobacco shop of Alderman James Kelly, who he suspected of rebel sympathies. He took Skeffington with him as a 'hostage' and ordered him to say his prayers. When Skeffington refused to do so, Bowen-Colthurst said his own prayer: 'Oh Lord, if it shall please Thee to take the life of this man forgive him for Christ's sake.'

Coming out onto Rathmines Road with his hostage in tow, Bowen-Colthurst and his party met two youths, Laurence Byrne and J.J. Coade, who were coming from a sodality meeting. After a brief interrogation, Bowen-Colthurst drew his pistol and shot Coade dead. The party proceeded to Kelly's shop and threw a grenade through the window. Kelly was absent, but two journalists – Thomas Dickson, who was Scottish and disabled, and Patrick MacIntyre – were arrested and taken back to the barracks, along with Skeffington. Neither man had any connection with the Rising.

Shortly after 10am on Wednesday morning, Bowen-Colthurst ordered that Skeffington, Dickson and MacIntyre be taken out to a yard beside the guardroom 'for the purpose of speaking to them'. He then summoned seven soldiers and ordered the three men to walk to a wall at the back of the yard. As the men turned to face him, Bowen-Colthurst ordered the soldiers to fire. The men fell, and the soldiers filed out. A lieutenant who heard the volley entered the yard and saw that, though the other two were clearly dead, Skeffington's leg was still twitching. When this was reported to Bowen-Colthurst, he ordered four soldiers to fire another volley into the body. The three bodies were wrapped in sheets and buried in the barrack square.

In June, Bowen-Colthurst was tried by court martial for the three murders. He was found guilty but insane, and committed to Broadmoor asylum.

Wimborne's declaration of martial law, as posted around Dublin on April 29th. It declares that 'certain evilly disposed persons and associations' have committed 'divers acts of violence'.

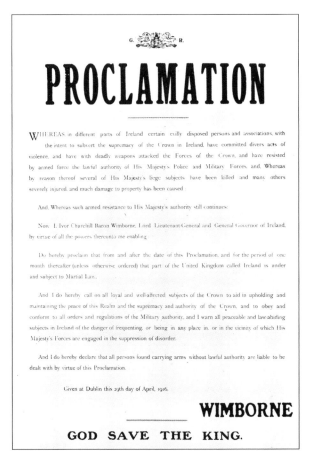

G. R.

PROCLAMATION

WHEREAS in different parts of Ireland certain evilly disposed persons and associations, with the intent to subvert the supremacy of the Crown in Ireland, have committed divers acts of violence, and have with deadly weapons attacked the Forces of the Crown, and have resisted by armed force the lawful authority of His Majesty's Police and Military Forces and, Whereas by reason thereof several of His Majesty's liege subjects have been killed and many others severely injured, and much damage to property has been caused:

And, Whereas such armed resistance to His Majesty's authority still continues:

Now I, Ivor Churchill Baron Wimborne, Lord Lieutenant-General and General Governor of Ireland, by virtue of all the powers thereunto me enabling:

Do hereby proclaim that from and after the date of this Proclamation, and for the period of one month thereafter (unless otherwise ordered) that part of the United Kingdom called Ireland is under and subject to Martial Law.

And I do hereby call on all loyal and well-affected subjects of the Crown to aid in upholding and maintaining the peace of this Realm and the supremacy and authority of the Crown, and to obey and conform to all orders and regulations of the Military authority, and I warn all peaceable and law-abiding subjects in Ireland of the danger of frequenting, or being in any place in, or in the vicinity of which His Majesty's Forces are engaged in the suppression of disorder.

And I do hereby declare that all persons found carrying arms without lawful authority are liable to be dealt with by virtue of this Proclamation.

Given at Dublin this 29th day of April, 1916.

WIMBORNE

GOD SAVE THE KING.

'Although we saw, from our position, very few soldiers, some few, whom we could not see, kept up an intermittent sniping at us. Several bullets entered the rooms we occupied, and, presumably, a number lodged in the leather-bound volumes with which we had most of the windows barricaded. One of these bullets passed through the wooden casing of my rifle, just in front of the first finger of my left hand, without injuring either the finger or the barrel of the rifle. Where that bullet was fired from, we could only guess, but it certainly came from a sniper who had got our range, was not too far away, and which was probably provided with field glasses which aided him in sighting our loop-hole.'

The rebels in St Stephen's Green were also experiencing the realities of war. At daybreak, the government soldiers who had slipped into the Shelbourne Hotel opened fire on them with a machine gun. The thick vegetation saved them from horrific casualties, but their position was untenable and by noon they had withdrawn to the College of Surgeons.

British troops man a barricade on Talbot Street. Barricades were generally make-shift affairs, with a selection of chairs and sofas used to bolster this one.

James Stephens noticed that 'inside the Green railings four bodies could be seen lying on the ground. They were dead Volunteers. Some distance beyond the Shelbourne I saw another Volunteer stretched out on a seat just within the railings. He was not dead, for, now and again, his hand moved feebly in a gesture for aid; the hand was completely red with blood. His face could not be seen. He was just a limp mass, upon which the rain beat pitilessly, and he was sodden and shapeless, and most miserable to see.'

Nevil Norway also saw this dying man. As his mother wrote, 'After the Green had been raked by our machine-gun fire, he strolled up, in his casual way, to see the result! ... Lying full-length on the seat, face downwards, was a man, a civilian, with his lower jaw blown away and bleeding profusely. N. immediately climbed the railings and dropped down on the Sinn

Féin side and found that the man was still living; he then turned and fairly cursed the men who were looking on, and asked if there was not one man enough to come over the railings and help him. Whereupon three men climbed over and together they lifted down the seat with the poor creature lying on it … they were able to open the gate, and then brought out the seat and the man on it and carried him to the nearest hospital, where he died in about five minutes.'

Inside City Hall, Helena Molony and her comrades had been coming under sustained attack from artillery and machine guns since the early hours of the morning. As the troops stormed City Hall, she heard a window smash at the back of the building 'and then we knew they were pouring in … A voice said "Surrender, in the name of the King." At this point I felt a pluck on my arm and our youngest girl, Annie Norgrove … said to me "Miss Molony, Miss Molony, we are not going to give in? Mr Connolly said we were not to surrender." She was terrified, but there was no surrender about her.'

As the soldiers continued to pour in, however, the defenders were overwhelmed. Helena Molony and her female comrades were the cause of some confusion to the troops. 'The British officers thought these girls had been taken prisoner by the rebels. They asked them "Did they do anything to you? Were they kind to you? How many are up here?" Jinny Shanahan, quick enough, answered: "No, they did not do anything to us. There are hundreds upstairs – big guns and everything." She invented such a story that they thought there was a garrison up on the roof, with the result that they did delay and took precautions. It was not until the girls were brought out for safety and, apparently, when they were bringing down some of the men, that one of the lads said "Hullo, Jinny, are you all right?" The officer looked at her, angry, the way he was fooled by this girl.' Helena Molony and the other women were then led to a dirty barrack room on the Ship Street side of the castle and imprisoned.

In the afternoon, the *Daily Express* building on Cork Hill, which served as an outpost to the rebel detachment in City Hall, was also stormed by troops. From Trinity College, John

British soldiers using casks as cover for the fire, although this picture is believed to be among those posed immediately after the Rising and not taken during the battle itself. Note the pile of fish heads in the lower left corner.

REPORTERS BARRED FROM THE ACTION

The Irish Journalist noted mordantly that the reporting of the Rising was a comparatively safe affair. 'Journalists after the second day were not allowed by the military to venture into the firing line. It was, perhaps, just as well, as Dublin reporters have never been paid the salaries of war correspondents. They were not, in fact, permitted to pass the military cordons for some days after the suppression of the revolt. They were then provided with special permits and, on the whole, did excellent work, having regard to the obstacles with which they were confronted at every hand's turn.'

SUB-EDITOR 'ONLY JOURNALIST TO DIE'

According to *The Irish Journalist*, the only journalist to die in the Rising was a sub-editor. 'We desire to extend our sympathy to the relatives of Mr P. Reynolds, of the *Evening Mail* sub-editorial staff, who received three bullet wounds in Dame Street on Easter Monday and succumbed to his injuries in Mercer's Hospital ...' Clearly this did not include the two journalists shot with Francis Sheehy Skeffington.

Joly watched in confusion: 'We were at the time in ignorance of what was actually happening; for we were possessed with the idea that the Sinn Féiners held the Castle. When, therefore, we saw at the head of Dame Street men in successive waves rush across the street from the City Hall towards the "Express" offices, we thought they represented the enemy in process of expulsion from the Castle. As a matter of fact the waves of men were composed of the troops. From our position in front of the College we could see that a terrific fire was being directed against the *Daily Express* building: plaster and powdered brick were flying in showers from its facade. This fire was to cover the advance of our soldiers. But in spite of this we saw, more than once, one of the running figures pitch forward and fall ... The fight seemed to last a considerable time – about an hour at its greatest intensity – before the firing began to wane.'

As these reverses were being experienced by the rebels, Robert Holland was also getting his first piece of bad news. A Volunteer, Jack Saul, told him that 'he had been with Captain T. McCarthy who had mysteriously disappeared and that the whole garrison had left. This garrison had taken over Roe's distillery at the top of Mount Brown and James's Street and opposite to the South Dublin Union front entrance gate.' More cheering was the arrival both of six chickens which a rebel-supporting messenger-boy had been meant to deliver to the officers' mess at Richmond Barracks but had instead diverted to the Volunteers, and of a birthday cake which his mother had sent from home.

Even as the authorities were beginning to pick off these rebel detachments, however, Dublin was still buzzing with rumours of a vast uprising. Real news was at a premium. *The Irish Times* appeared on the streets, but its extensive reports of the previous day's events had been suppressed and it carried just two references to the Rising. One was a proclamation from the Lord Lieutenant, Lord Wimborne, announcing

Constance Markievicz (on left), seen here with her sister Eva Gore-Booth. A member of the Irish Citizen Army and founder of the militaristic scout movement Na Fianna Éireann, Markievicz became a key icon of the 1916 Rising.

'PRESSMEN' AT THE SHARP END

A number of journalists were caught up in the Rising, as rebels, civilians or 'counter revolutionaries'. *The Irish Journalist*, the organ of the Irish Journalists Association, offers a fascinating insight into the time.

The issue for May and August 1916 records that the association's offices in Middle Abbey Street were destroyed in the fighting. It goes on: 'The loss of our Secretary (Mr Pierce Beazley) who has been sentenced to three years' penal servitude for his participation in the Rising has had an injurious effect on our Organisation.'

It notes that 'numbers of other equally brilliant young pressmen and literary men' were arrested after the Rising. Those listed include Robert Brennan from Enniscorthy, Co. Wexford, (later the Irish ambassador to the United States, and father of writer Maeve Brennan); William Sears, editor of the *Enniscorthy Echo*; Arthur Griffith, editor of Nationality; Michael Knightley of the *Irish Independent*; Brian O'Higgins; and Herbert Pim, editor of *The Irishman*.

'Had an Irish Republic been established we have been informed that four journalists would have been asked to answer a charge of high treason, so whether the volunteers won or lost in their fight against the forces of the British Government some Pressmen were bound to suffer at the hands of one side or another.'

Children set about the rubble looking for firewood. This was an innocent pursuit, compared to the many other men and women who engaged in widespread looting of shops during the breakdown of law and order, often at great risk to their lives.

SUNDAY
23

MONDAY
24

TUESDAY
25

WEDNESDAY
26

THURSDAY
27

FRIDAY
28

SATURDAY
29

an attempt 'to incite rebellion' by 'a reckless, though small, body of men' and warning that 'the sternest measures' were being taken. The other was a tiny report, containing fewer than 50 words, beginning, 'Yesterday morning an insurrectionary rising took place in the city of Dublin.'

The vacuum was filled with rumour. James Stephens 'met a wild individual who spat rumour as though his mouth were a machine gun or a linotype machine. He believed everything he heard; and everything he heard became as by magic favourable to his hopes, which were violently anti-English ... He said the Germans had landed in three places. One of these landings alone consisted of fifteen thousand men. The other landings probably beat that figure. The whole City of Cork was in the hands of the Volunteers, and, to that extent, might be said to be peaceful. German warships had defeated the English, and their transports were speeding from every side. The whole country was up, and the garrison was out-numbered by one hundred to one. Those Dublin barracks which had not been taken were now besieged and on the point of surrender.'

O'Connell Street, where there was only sporadic shooting, was still a surreal site. Francis Sheehy Skeffington had printed leaflets condemning looting and asking for volunteers for a civic police force, but his efforts were unavailing. People were selling looted diamond rings and gold watches for sixpence or a shilling. Ernie O'Malley watched as 'Kiddies carried golf bags and acted as caddies as young gentlemen in bright football jerseys and tall hats, hit golf balls with their clubs, or indeed anything else.' A young girl passed him with a fan in her hand and a gold bracelet on her wrist. 'She wore a sable fur coat, the pockets overhung with stockings and pale pink drawers: on her head was a wide black hat to which she had pinned streamers of blue silk ribbon. She strutted in larkish delight calling to others less splendid: "How do yez like me now?"'

At 4.10pm, Eamon Bulfin on the roof of the GPO, watched as children looted a photography and toy shop, Lawrence's, and came out with a large quantity of fireworks. They 'made a huge pile of them in the middle of O'Connell Street, and set fire to them. That is one thing that will stick in my mind forever. We had our bombs on top of the Post Office, and these fireworks were shooting up in the sky. We were very nervous. There were catherine wheels going up O'Connell Street and catherine wheels coming down O'Connell Street.' The looters then set Lawrence's on fire.

After dark, Robert Holland slipped over the wall of Jameson's distillery and met up with his young brother Walter and another boy, to strip equipment from the bodies of dead soldiers. 'We crawled into Fairbrother's Field and made very slow progress and the time seemed very long before we picked out the first dead soldier. I cut off his web equipment and one of the others took his rifle. In this manner we stripped quite a lot of dead soldiers. In all we got five rifles ... We tied the web equipment on us and found it very hard to crawl along the ground and not make noise.' They got the equipment back to the distillery, then went back for more. When he eventually got back to his post, Jack Saul told him that he thought he had heard digging underneath them. Holland listened and heard 'this noise, like chains rattling. Something very heavy was being moved about. Saul shouted out "Halt!" but the movement still went on. I shouted "Halt or I fire!" and we both shouted that we had it covered. We then decided to fire at the gate. Both of us fired and then a lot of confusion and noise ensued.' A few minutes later, they discovered that they had shot a horse.

Thomas Walsh and his brother Jim, who had both been with Éamon de Valera in Boland's mill, were sent to reinforce the small garrison at Clanwilliam House, overlooking Mount Street Bridge. After dark, when Thomas was about to leave one of the rooms in the house, 'I saw what I thought was a man hiding, and I called "Hands up" twice. On the third challenge I still got no reply and switched on the torch. You can imagine my surprise at finding it to be a dressmaker's model!'

But the mad carnival of the streets and the comedy of mistaken identity could turn deadly at any moment. During the evening, one of Captain Gerrard's sentries at Beggar's Bush approached him. '"I beg your pardon, Sir, I have just shot two girls." I said, "What on earth did you do that for?" He said, "I thought they were rebels. I was told they were dressed in all classes of attire." At a range of about 200 yards I saw two girls – about twenty – lying dead.'

THE FIGHTING INTENSIFIES

Wednesday, April 26th

- At 8am, the shelling of an empty Liberty Hall begins.

- Rebels holding out in the Mendicity Institute, near the Four Courts, surrender after ammunition finally runs out.

- British troops continue landing at Kingstown (now Dún Laoghaire). The public welcomes soldiers by giving them food as they march towards the city.

- At Mount Street Bridge rebels engage these troops. In a battle that lasts until evening, there are heavy government casualties.

- Fires begin to spread on O'Connell Street. General Sir John Grenfell Maxwell is dispatched from London to deal with the Rising.

- Heavy fighting between Ypres and Souchez on the Western Front.

After a night of continuous firing, Dublin woke to another day of sunshine, and to the sound of shelling. The gunboat *Helga* had sailed up the Liffey and, at the stroke of 8am, it began shelling Liberty Hall. The first shell missed, and struck the bridge behind it, but subsequent shells destroyed the building, which was empty after its only occupant – its caretaker – had fled. From her home on Dawson Street, Arthur Hamilton Norway's wife Mary Louisa heard the bombardment. 'It made me feel quite sick,' she wrote.

In the morning, James Stephens took a walk to St Stephen's Green, where rebels sniped from the roof of the College of Surgeons. However, government troops now had machine guns on the roofs of three buildings on the Green – the Shelbourne Hotel, the United Service Club, and the Alexandra Club – and a duel had opened up across the trees.

'Through the railings of the Green some rifles and bandoliers could be seen lying on the ground, as also the deserted trenches and snipers' holes,' Stephens recalled. 'Small boys bolted in to see these sights and bolted out again with bullets quickening their feet. Small boys do not believe that people will really kill them, but small boys were killed.'

A proclamation of martial law had been posted throughout the city, warning people to stay indoors between 7pm and 5am. However, Stephens described a good mood among Dubliners. 'Almost everyone was smiling and attentive, and a democratic feeling was abroad, to which our city is very much a stranger; for while in private we are a sociable and talkative people we have no street manners or public ease whatever. Every person spoke to every other person, and men and women mixed and talked without constraint.'

Opinion among civilians was divided, although women were far less sympathetic to the rebels than the men, according to Stephens. 'Most of the female opinion I heard was not alone unfavourable but actively and viciously hostile to the rising. This was noticeable among the best-dressed class of our population; the worst-dressed, indeed the female dregs of Dublin life, expressed a like antagonism, and almost in similar language. The view expressed was, "I hope every man of them will be shot." And, "They ought to be all shot."'

On O'Connell Street, Eamon Bulfin witnessed the day begin with an unusual, and tragic, episode. 'There was a tram upturned at Earl Street and in the middle of all this shooting, scurrying and general tumult, we heard a voice shout: "I'm a bloody Dublin Fusilier. I don't give a damn about anyone." He staggered out into the middle of O'Connell Street where he was riddled with machine gun fire. One of our men, with a white flag, went over to the where he lay, knelt down, said a prayer over his body and dragged him in to the side.'

Having spent the first days of the Rising waiting with a garrison in the northern suburb of Fairview, Oscar Traynor's men had finally been ordered to move to the GPO. About 60 men in all had gathered their equipment and materials – which included more weapons than personnel – and begun marching towards the city centre late on Tuesday. Along the way, they captured some British soldiers, although this was to cause some trouble when, upon reaching O'Connell Street, the group was told to move across the street to the GPO.

'The volunteers were then sent across in single file, taking with them a number of British soldiers who had been taken prisoner and who were in full khaki dress, which resulted in a rather extraordinary incident,' according to Traynor's account. 'As this single file of

As Easter week progressed, troops began to arrive from Britain in an attempt to bolster the units already based in Ireland. As did the rebels, they had to contend with the curiosity of the public.

volunteers and British soldiers were doubling across the road, fire was opened on them from the Imperial Hotel, which was occupied by our own men. In the course of the firing, James Connolly rushed out into the street with his hands over his head, shouting towards the Imperial Hotel. Immediately following his appearance the firing ceased, but not before a couple of our men had been wounded. Connolly returned to our men, said: "It is all a mistake". He then ushered us into the GPO where we were formed up and were addressed by Patrick Pearse, standing upon a table.'

He commended them on their actions, and told them: 'You will find victory, even though that victory may be found in death.' For Traynor, 'that was another terribly thrilling moment'.

Members of Dublin Fire Brigade in 1916.

Traynor was then sent to oversee the fortifying of the Metropole Hotel. 'When this was completed, I reported in person to James Connolly in the GPO and informed him of what we had done. He then accompanied me to the Metropole Hotel, went through the building, examined all the positions, examined the holes which we had dug, made an effort to get through one of these holes and got through with some difficulty. I followed Connolly through the hole in the wall, and he said to me: "I wouldn't like to be getting through that hole if the enemy were following me with bayonets". I then reminded him that these holes were built according to instructions issued to him in the course of his lectures.

'We reached Easons in Abbey Street and, although at this time heavy firing was taking place, Connolly insisted on walking into Abbey Street and giving me instructions as to where I should place the barricade. While he was giving instructions, he was standing on the edge of the path and the bullets were actually striking the pavements around us.

'I pointed this out to him and said that I thought it was a grave risk to be taking and that these instructions could be given inside. He came back, absolutely unperturbed, to Easons with me, and while we were standing in the portico of Easons a shell struck a building opposite – I think it was the Catholic Boys' Home – and caused a gaping hole to appear in the front of the house. Connolly jokingly remarked: "They don't appear to be satisfied with firing bullets at us, they are firing shells now."'

Connolly returned to the GPO, while Traynor and his men settled into their position at the Metropole Hotel. The shelling continued.

'They were shrapnel shells, and the amazing thing was that instead of bullets coming in it was molten lead, actually molten, which streamed about on the ground when it fell. I was told that the shrapnel was filled with molten wax, the bullets were embedded in wax, and the velocity of the shell through the barrel and through the air caused the mould to melt. As the first of those shells hit the house, the volunteers rushed and told me about them. I rushed up and found an old fellow crawling about on his hands and knees gathering the stuff up as it hardened. I asked him what he was doing and what he intended to do with the stuff. He said "Souvenirs". That is all he said.

'From this time onwards the shelling continued, and the building was hit on a number of occasions, the chimney-stack falling in as a result of one of these explosions.'

At 2pm, the GPO shook. The rebels were unsure what it was. 'Some say that a bomb had exploded in the lower room,' remembered Volunteer Dick Humphreys. 'Others say it is a dynamite explosion, but a second and third in quick succession prove the correctness of those who proclaimed it heavy artillery.

'The detonations were truly tremendous, and were we not absolutely certain that the gun was situated on the other side of the river, one could have sworn that it was at least in Abbey Street. For a time the men were uneasy at this their first experience of heavy gun-fire, but soon they become accustomed to the sound, and take no more notice of it than of the ordinary rifle fire.'

At Marrowbone Lane, Robert Holland could hear the explosions in the distance. While it would be a quieter day for the rebels at his position (being an apprentice butcher, in the morning he was asked to slaughter a cow for meat) he described one unusual episode. 'I noticed that a woman that I had seen the day before leaning out of a window opposite me.

'THERE WAS WHAT THEY CALL A FAIRLY SHARP FIRE FIGHT ...'

Capt. E. Gerrard was in Beggar's Bush Barracks on the day of the battle at Mount Street Bridge.

'At about four o'clock on Wednesday afternoon some of the Sherwood Foresters arrived in Beggars Bush Barracks – 25 – as far as I can remember, untrained, undersized products of the English slums. Sir Frederick Shaw said to me – we were being very badly sniped from the railway bridge, South Lotts Road – "You take QM Gamble and those men, climb up the railway line and put them off." I said, "Very good, Sir."'

He mentions that 'the young Sherwoods that I had with me had never fired a service rifle before. They were not even able to load them. We had to show them how to load them.

'We got over the side of the Barracks and through the houses on Shelbourne Road and up on to the railway by a ladder. I was over the wall first, followed by QM Sergeant Gamble. As soon as I got over the wall, at a range of about 200 yards, about eight Sinn Féiners advanced from the direction of the city to meet us. I saw them coming towards us firing. There was what they call a fairly sharp fire fight. These men were standing up, not lying down. They came out of their trenches to meet us. They were very brave, I remember. They did not know how many of us there might be. The first casualty was QM Gamble. He was shot dead, under the right eye. I was the next casualty. I don't know how many Sherwoods were killed. One of them was wounded on the approach to the railway.'

The wounded Capt. Gerrard was taken to Portobello Hospital, where he saw Capt. Bowen-Colthurst 'raging along the perimeter of the walls. Even then I was told he was quite mad'. He concludes: 'When I was in hospital, the soldiers used to come in and say how many they had shot. These were Irish troops – Irishmen. They were not like the Sherwood Foresters.'

A St John's Ambulance Brigade inspection just after the 1916 Rising. Most of those killed and wounded during the rebellion were civilians.

Liberty Hall lies in ruins after it was targeted by the gunship Helga. *Across the city, people heard the bombardment begin at 8am on Wednesday. After the first shell missed, striking the bridge behind it, subsequent shells destroyed the building, which was empty once its caretaker had fled.*

She had a hat, blouse and apron on her and I got suspicious.' He told a fellow Volunteer, Mick O'Callaghan, that he was going to shoot at her. 'He said "No". I said it was a queer place for a woman to be and that it was queer she should have a hat on her, as she must have seen the bullets flying around but took no notice of them. I made up my mind. She was only 35 or 40 yards away from me and I fired at her. She sagged half way out the window. The hat and small shawl fell off her and I saw what I took to be a woman was a man in his shirt sleeves.'

The interior of Liberty Hall after it was shelled. It was badly damaged as some of the shells exploded inside the building.

At the Mendicity Institute, at Usher's Quay, rebels were holding up the movement of soldiers between Kingsbridge train station and the city, while also protecting the Four Courts garrison.

Among those on the government side was an Australian private, John Joseph Chapman, who had actually arrived in Ireland on holiday. He was on convalescence leave, having spent three months at Gallipoli until illness forced his evacuation. With friends, he had been sightseeing, horse riding and boating on the lakes of Killarney before returning to Dublin on

GUINNESS WORKERS KILLED BY SOLDIERS

The many serious incidents during the week included the shooting dead of a number of Guinness workers by government soldiers, according to a contemporary report in the *Weekly Irish Times*.

'William John Rice, a night clerk in the Guinness brewery, along with Lieut A. Lucas of the 2nd King Edwards horse regiment, was shot dead at his place of work, by members of the Royal Dublin Fusiliers, on Friday, April 28th. It appears the two men were making their nightly round of the brewery buildings when they were challenged by very nervous and jumpy Royal Dubliners. The soldiers later claimed they had caught Sinn Féiners infiltrating the brewery premises, and shot them. Another officer and a civilian brewery employee, Lieut Worswick and Mr Dockeray, also a Guinness worker, were shot dead around the same time.

'These deaths caused considerable concern as the victims were known not to have any sympathy for the rebel cause. Company Quarter Master Sergeant Robert Flood was subsequently court-martialled for the first two deaths. In evidence for the defence it was argued that

Seán Heuston, who led three dozen rebels against 400 British soldiers from the Mendicity Institute, at Usher's Quay, holding up the troops' advance from Kingsbridge Station to the Four Courts. The railway station would later be renamed Heuston Station in his honour.

Easter Monday. Arriving at Kingsbridge Station he was immediately ordered to be ready for duty, and by Wednesday morning found himself in a firefight with rebels who were led by the man after whom Kingsbridge Station would later be renamed – Seán Heuston. 'Given rifle and ammunition and had to fight enemy in the streets,' Chapman noted in his diary. 'Nearly got hit several times. Only a few casualties on our side.'

Heuston's men, numbering three dozen, were holding out against an estimated 400 government soldiers and the fighting was at close quarters, sometimes as close as 20ft. The government forces began lobbing hand grenades into the building, which the rebels would occasionally throw back at them. Gradually, the rebels began to run out of ammunition, suffered casualties and were threatened with being over-run. Eventually, and despite the protestations of some of his men, Heuston decided that surrender was the only option. The Mendicity Institute garrison became the first to surrender its position without being overrun.

The third day of the Rising, however, would be remembered for a bloody battle that centred on Mount Street Bridge, to the south of the city.

The handful of rebels dispersed between 25 Northumberland Road, the road's schools and Clanwilliam House had had a quiet night, but in Clanwilliam House Thomas Walsh was tired after keeping watch. At 7am, he and his brother Jim were allowed a couple of hours sleep, and then some breakfast. At 10am, they began barricading a window when they spotted a neighbour of theirs passing the house. The Walshes asked him to tell their mother that they were alive and to send some food.

Over the course of the night and the morning, British troops had been arriving at Kingstown (Dún Laoghaire). They had lost one of their four machine guns while embarking in England, and had also left all their grenades behind. Two of the machine guns were then sent to Arklow, where there were reports of trouble.

Lucas and Rice had shown signs of Sinn Féin sympathies.

The judge was quick to point out that no such evidence had been produced in the case of Lucas. The managing director of Guinness issued a statement saying, on behalf of the company, that neither Rice nor Dockeray 'was in any way connected with, or in sympathy with the Sinn Féin rebellion'.

In the event the accused man was acquitted. 'The result was received with applause in court', the *Weekly Irish Times* reported, having devoted much space to an issue which, like the shooting of Francis Sheehy Skeffington, clearly troubled many of its readers.

At 10.35am, four battalions of the Sherwood Foresters marched towards the city. Most were in uniform no longer than eight weeks, and many had never fired a rifle. As they walked through the south Dublin sunshine, many of them presumed that they were in France.

The battalions split, with two heading for Kilmainham. The others continued towards the city centre. Greeted with tea and sandwiches by Dubliners, maps and field glasses were pressed into their hands as gifts, and intelligence of varying accuracy was given to them regarding the rebels' position.

One battalion adjutant, Capt. Frederick Dietrichsen, had the surprise of seeing and stopping to embrace with his wife, Beatrice, and children in the crowd. They had fled to Dublin from their Nottingham home in fear of German Zeppelin raids.

A few minutes later, the Sherwood Foresters encountered the rebels. Capt. Dietrichsen was amongst the first to die.

Some 300 yards from Mount Street Bridge, the troops came under fire from 25 Northumberland Road. Ten Sherwood Foresters fell in that volley. After some confusion, they identified the source of the firing, but without heavy guns to support them, officers drew their swords and led a bayonet charge across the road and towards the rebels' house, where they were shot at point-blank range.

In Clanwilliam House, Thomas and Jim Walsh had received a parcel sent by their mother, and carried by their brother Leo. 'We let down the rope and he tied it to the parcel. But while doing so he was fired upon and had to take cover in the garden.

'While hauling up the parcel, the rope snapped and fell into the area below. Leo got down and tied it on again and we got it up safely this time. The parcel contained steak (hot), bread, butter, etc, also a note telling us how proud they, at home, were of the news from all parts of Dublin, and not to be worrying about them.

'The entire garrison set to work on the steak, etc, and we made a good job of it. They were George Reynolds, Jimmy Doyle, Paddy Doyle, Dick Murphy, Willie Ronan, Jim and myself. We were nearly finished the meal when we heard firing not far off and we all rushed to our posts.'

He and Jim were positioned at the back of the house. 'It was now about 12 noon. I saw a man in English uniform running from Percy Lane along Percy Place and up the steps of a house. I fired for the first time from my Howth gun, and for that matter from any other rifle!

A poster asking Irishmen to sign up for the war by appealing to any notions of revenge after the sinking of the Lusitania *in May 1915. By early 1916, 146,000 Irish were in the British Army.*

POBLACHT NA H EIREANN.

THE PROVISIONAL GOVERNMENT
OF THE
IRISH REPUBLIC
TO THE PEOPLE OF IRELAND.

IRISHMEN AND IRISHWOMEN : In the name of God and of the dead generations from which she receives her old tradition of nationhood, Ireland, through us, summons her children to her flag and strikes for her freedom.

Having organised and trained her manhood through her secret revolutionary organisation, the Irish Republican Brotherhood, and through her open military organisations, the Irish Volunteers and the Irish Citizen Army, having patiently perfected her discipline, having resolutely waited for the right moment to reveal itself, she now seizes that moment, and, supported by her exiled children in America and by gallant allies in Europe, but relying in the first on her own strength, she strikes in full confidence of victory.

We declare the right of the people of Ireland to the ownership of Ireland, and to the unfettered control of Irish destinies, to be sovereign and indefeasible. The long usurpation of that right by a foreign people and government has not extinguished the right, nor can it ever be extinguished except by the destruction of the Irish people. In every generation the Irish people have asserted their right to national freedom and sovereignty ; six times during the past three hundred years they have asserted it in arms. Standing on that fundamental right and again asserting it in arms in the face of the world, we hereby proclaim the Irish Republic as a Sovereign Independent State, and we pledge our lives and the lives of our comrades-in-arms to the cause of its freedom, of its welfare, and of its exaltation among the nations.

The Irish Republic is entitled to, and hereby claims, the allegiance of every Irishman and Irishwoman. The Republic guarantees religious and civil liberty, equal rights and equal opportunities to all its citizens, and declares its resolve to pursue the happiness and prosperity of the whole nation and of all its parts, cherishing all the children of the nation equally, and oblivious of the differences carefully fostered by an alien government, which have divided a minority from the majority in the past.

Until our arms have brought the opportune moment for the establishment of a permanent National Government, representative of the whole people of Ireland and elected by the suffrages of all her men and women, the Provisional Government, hereby constituted, will administer the civil and military affairs of the Republic in trust for the people.

We place the cause of the Irish Republic under the protection of the Most High God, Whose blessing we invoke upon our arms, and we pray that no one who serves that cause will dishonour it by cowardice, inhumanity, or rapine. In this supreme hour the Irish nation must, by its valour and discipline and by the readiness of its children to sacrifice themselves for the common good, prove itself worthy of the august destiny to which it is called.

Signed on Behalf of the Provisional Government,

THOMAS J. CLARKE,

SEAN Mac DIARMADA,   THOMAS MacDONAGH,

P. H. PEARSE,   EAMONN CEANNT,

JAMES CONNOLLY.   JOSEPH PLUNKETT.

The Proclamation of the Irish Republic, read by Patrick Pearse outside the GPO on Easter Monday. It is assumed that Pearse wrote a draft, with additions by James Connolly and other signatories, but nobody knows for certain. About 2,500 copies were either posted about the street or left to be taken away by on-lookers.

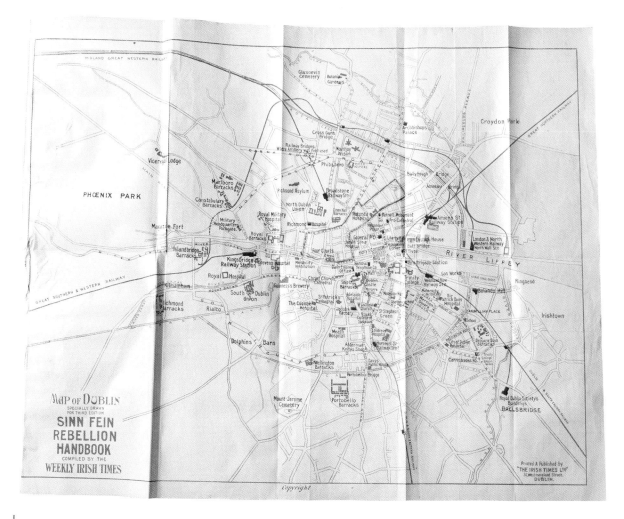

A map of Dublin, featuring the main flashpoints of the rebellion, which was later published in the Weekly Irish Times Sinn Féin Rebellion Handbook.

One of the two flags flown by the rebels from the roof of the GPO. This bore the words 'Irish Republic' against a green background, while the other was a tricolour. They were flown in place of the Union Jack.

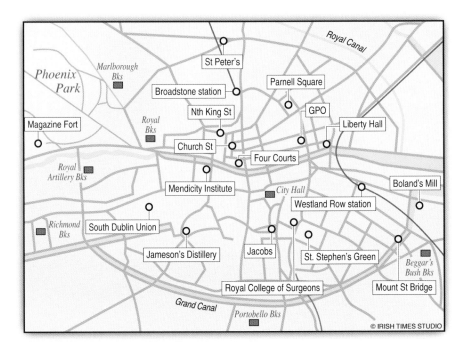

A map showing how the four Dublin battalions were deployed throughout the city.

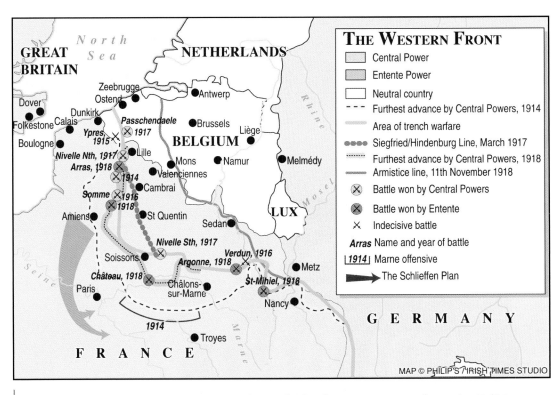

A map of the Western Front, on which tens of thousands of Irish men were serving during the 1916 Rising. On the Thursday alone, 538 men died during a gas attack on the 16th (Irish) Division, more than that in the entire week of the Rising.

A plaque at 16 Moore Street marking the spot where the rebels set up their headquarters as they fled the burning GPO. It was from this building that Patrick Pearse is believed to have seen the death of three elderly men, and decided to surrender so as to stop the carnage.

The Record of the Irish Rebellion, *a special edition of* Irish Life *published after the events of Easter Week. Its rather dramatic cover illustrates the inferno which engulfed O'Connell Street.*

Pearse's handwritten note of surrender from the Sunday, when groups of rebels were continuing to fight, unaware of the changed situation elsewhere.

A cross marks the spot in the Stonebreaker's Yard of Kilmainham Gaol, where the executions took place.

Some mementoes of the 1916 Rising. Relics of the event today fetch considerable sums at auction.

A post-First World War map of the world, showing the British Empire in red.

An imaginative recreation of the GPO Garrison by Thomas Ryan, RHA.

Mount Street Bridge, where a small band of rebels inflicted severe casualties on the Sherwood Foresters. Newly trained in trench warfare, the soldiers attacked in waves until the dead and injured piled up on the bridge.

I do not know what happened to me, or how long I was unconscious. In the excitement I did not heed the lectures and did not hold the weapon correctly. The result was, the butt hit me under the arm and knocked me out.'

Walsh came to his senses and 'fired again and again until the rifle heated so much it was impossible to hold it'.

He moved to another window. 'From here we could see terrible confusion among the enemy. They were being attacked from 25 Northumberland Road, held by Mick Malone and Jimmy Grace. Those who managed to get by "25" ran towards [Mount Street] Bridge and took cover anywhere they could find it, on house steps, behind trees, and even in the channels on the roadway. We kept on blazing away at those in the channels, and after a time

An ambulance races along a Dublin street. During the Mount Street battle, there would be lulls in fighting to allow for the collection of wounded, with both sides commenting on the gallantry of doctors and nurses.

as they were killed, the next fellow moved up and passed the man killed in front of him. This gave one the impression of a giant human khaki-coloured caterpillar.'

Newly trained in the tactics of trench warfare the Sherwood Foresters were refused permission to move around and flank the rebels, but ordered at the blow of a whistle to make a full frontal charge.

'They went down on the Bridge again, and again they made the attempt, but they did not survive. By now there was a great pile of dead and dying on the Bridge.'

A clergyman, and nurses and doctors from a nearby hospital, braved the shooting to remove the dead and dying. 'From the moment the first civilian got to the Bridge not one shot was fired by either side,' observed Walsh, 'and when the last civilian was out of sight the firing started again, and the Bridge was rushed as before but with the same result. Again the Bridge was filled with dead and dying, and again cleared by the civilians who now had white sheets to carry the wounded on.'

In Boland's mill, it seems that Éamon de Valera decided against reinforcing the rebels around Mount Street Bridge because he expected an assault on his own position. The rebels began to suffer casualties, as described by Thomas Walsh. 'During the latter fight Paddy Doyle would say, "Boys, isn't this a great day for Ireland?" and little sentences like this. He was very proud to live to see such a day. After some time Paddy was not saying anything. Jim spoke to him and got no reply. He pulled him by the coat and he fell over into his arms. He was shot through the head.'

Shortly after that, another Volunteer, Dick Murphy, was shot dead. Low on manpower, the rebels turned to the dressmaker's model that Thomas Walsh had found in the house. 'We put a coat on this and put it in front of the window (about six feet back in the room), and what a peppering this poor innocent thing got. It was riddled, but drew a lot of fire from our heads.'

A portrait of Éamon de Valera, who was leader of the garrison around Mount Street and Boland's mill, but who expected an attack on his position and did not send re-inforcements to the Mount Street rebels.

Dead and wounded littered the road. Occasionally, civilians attempted to escape the fighting. 'During the lull in the firing, while the cleaning-up process was on, an old man rushed from Percy Lane and was fired on from under the wall of the canal and fell dead. I heard after that he was an old German living in the neighbourhood.'

General Sir John Grenfell Maxwell with his staff in Dublin in 1916. On the Wednesday he was sent from London to take control of the worsening situation and given permission to use whatever means necessary.

One of the British soldiers that day, Sherwood Foresters Captain, Arthur Annan Dickson also noted the bravery of the hospital staff. 'Some wonderful nurses from a Dublin hospital appeared from ahead, walking into the thick of it and helping the wounded.'

A bank clerk with Lloyd's Bank, Dickson was a newly-commissioned officer experiencing his first taste of enemy fire. He had seen Capt. Dietrichsen greeting his wife and children just before the march took them into the firing line. 'Nearer Dublin we heard firing ahead and very high flames. Our C Company, spread out as advance-guard, came under fire near Ballsbridge from houses commanding our approach route.'

Dickson was sent forward. 'While there, shots came from a house in the road-fork just ahead; B Company under Major Hanson (seriously wounded just after) kept up covering fire on the house while I broke in with a few bayonet-men but the rebels left by the back way.'

Amid the chaos, Capt. Dickson had a lucky escape. 'I heard that my friend Hawken had been killed in attacking a house at a cross-road farther on. That house was blown in with bombs and the rebels gradually gave back from house to house as we advanced by rushes with some cover from trees along the kerbs, with bullets of all sorts chipping pavements and gate-posts; one chipped the bark one side of a tree as I left it.

'Another must have ricochetted off the pavement and struck end-on into my Field Service Pocket Book in a side pocket, but I never noticed it till afterwards.'

As the day wore on, newly arrived grenades and a machine gun began to turn the tide in favour of the British troops.

'We had to bomb a school building that the rebels were holding, and one of my men, Irvine, did some good throwing, right through the windows. A tall house beyond the bridge was commanding our further advance; it was rushed by Foster, senior subaltern of D Company; their bombs set the gas alight and burnt the house out. Opposition died down after that.'

In No. 25 Michael Malone was killed, and Jimmy Grace escaped. The schools were over-run. At Clanwilliam House, Thomas Walsh and the other rebels had spent their ammunition. They decided to evacuate. 'The house was smouldering in several places, the smoke and fumes were shocking. It was now about an hour before dark. We realised that we could stay no longer, and prepared to leave. While doing so, poor Reynolds stood up on the drawing-room landing to fire the last shot. Whether he got his man or not we did not know, but he fell dead in our midst.'

Walsh had no regrets over his role. 'The casualties were so great that I, at one time, thought we had accounted for the whole British Army in Ireland. What a thought! What joy! What a day! But a lot of their losses was their own fault. They made for sitting ducks for amateur riflemen. But they were brave men and, I must say, clean fighters.'

FOOD SHORTAGE ON NORTHSIDE

The north Dublin suburbs were badly affected by military restrictions on traffic. From Wednesday they were cut off from all communication with the city. A clash between insurgents and the Dublin Fusiliers on Tuesday night led to the erection of barricades, according to the *Weekly Irish Times*.

Access to Glasnevin Road from the North Circular Road was blocked, as was Cross Guns Bridge, Whitworth Road and Finglas Road.

People in Phibsborough were kept behind a cordon, and by Thursday 'something approaching a food famine was imminent'. People panicked, shops in the district were besieged and the flour mills at Cross Guns Bridge was targeted. 'Men and women of all classes were seen carrying away parcels of flour potatoes bread and everything ... in the way of foodstuffs.' Soon all the shops were cleared, the newspaper reported.

Making their escape, Walsh, his brother and the other surviving rebels made their way to the basement from where they climbed through a window and made their way over walls and through the lanes.

'There was a house with an open door and we went into the hall, where we met a girl and asked her to give us a coat or overcoat to put over our uniforms, she called to the mother and told her there were Volunteers at the door who wanted a change of clothing. The mother shouted down to her, "Put them out, put them out, we will all be shot." We did not trouble them further.'

Further along their journey, they met resistance from locals. 'The "Soldiers' Wives" had a lot of choice names for us, but our revolvers had a rather quietening effect.' However, they received clothes and food from other locals, before eventually being given shelter and a meal at a factory on Baggot Street, where they settled in for the night.

(It would be the beginning of a lengthy period on the run. It was November when Thomas and Jim Walsh returned to their parents' home, where they stayed indoors until December. With the release of the rebels from the internment camp at Frongoch that month, the Walshes finally concluded that it was time that they were 'released' too.)

Back on Lower Mount Street, the Sherwood Foresters' commanding officer Colonel Maconchy arrived to survey the scene. He was met with cheering crowds. In total, though, 230 British troops had been killed or wounded in the battle.

With the rebellion now going into its fourth day, General Sir John Maxwell was sent from London to take control of the worsening situation. His orders were to 'take such measures as may in your opinion be necessary for the prompt suppression of the insurrection'. In other words, he was to suppress the Rising using whatever means necessary.

CITY CENTRE UP
IN FLAMES

Thursday, April 27th

- In the GPO Connolly is wounded.

- The Four Courts and North King Street rebels are attacked, with fierce house-to-house fighting.

- There is a gun battle at the South Dublin Union (now St James's Hospital).

- Government troops use Guinness lorries as improvised armoured vehicles.

- Looting continues.

- Clery's and the Imperial Hotel crash to the ground as the centre of Dublin burns.

- At Hulluch on the Western Front, the 16th Irish Division sustains a horrific gas attack and suffers heavy casualties.

At Trinity College, Thursday morning brought the site of the university doubling as an army barracks.

'The quadrangles presented an extraordinary appearance,' according to the account written soon after by John Joly, who was also attached to the Officer Training Corps.

'Some 4,000 troops were stationed in the college. Horses tied to the chains which enclosed the grass plots gave the place the appearance of a vast open-air stable or horse fair. Men stood in ranks or sprawled on pavements or on the doorsteps – anywhere – sometimes closely packed and fast asleep in every conceivable attitude. Many of them had put in a hard night's work.' These included men from the Sherwood Foresters, fresh from the fight at Mount Street.

SUNDAY
23

MONDAY
24

TUESDAY
25

WEDNESDAY
26

THURSDAY
27

FRIDAY
28

SATURDAY
29

'Not a few who had been through these nocturnal and diurnal operations told me that they would prefer being at the Front. At the Front, they said, you knew which direction from which you may expect a bullet. Here the enemy is all around you. He lurks in the dark passages and chimney stacks, and when at last you think you have hunted him down, you find yourself in possession of a peaceful citizen who gives some plausible reason for his presence.'

Along with dead soldiers brought into the college grounds, wounded and dying civilians were also arriving by horse-drawn ambulance.

'Then a little boy was brought in on a stretcher. He had been shot through the hand on Monday, and there was fear that the wound had become septic. The father accompanied him, but even in these circumstances was not admitted to the quadrangles. He told me that none of the family had tasted food since Monday night. The child looked very ill – too ill to cry or complain ... Hot tea was given to the little patient. There was a rapid revival. He thanked us in a voice which never rose above a whisper.'

For Dubliners, conditions were deteriorating. 'The people were starving. Food supplies had early been exhausted or the shops had been closed. Wages had ceased, for there were no employers and no work to do. But wages would not have helped; there was nothing to buy. Relief of the starving was begun by the officers of the Officer Training Corps. Later, on the Thursday, the Military Authorities humanely and wisely took the problem in hand. Stores were commandeered and warehouses opened, and the food distributed to the starving families. I heard that the people were so grateful they would do anything for the soldiers.'

Capt. A.A. Dickson, a bullet still lodged in his field book after the battle at Mount Street, was not among the Sherwood Foresters in Trinity College on this morning. Instead, his company had continued to patrol the area between Mount Street and Merrion Square. He had managed a brief rest in a house, but it was just before dawn when soldiers from the South Staffordshires relieved his company. 'We tramped back to near Ballsbridge and slept on the pavements in relays off duty till we had a chance of breakfast.

Smoking ruins in Earl Street, Dublin. From the Metropole Hotel, Oscar Traynor watched the fire spread along O'Connell Street and then engulf a whole block along this street.

97

The city in the immediate aftermath of the Rising, as seen from O'Connell Bridge. The flames of the burning buildings were visible well outside of the city.

'THERE THEY LAY … IN EVERY CONCEIVABLE POSTURE OF HUMAN AGONY'

On Thursday, just outside the German-held village of Hulluch, a mile north of Loos, in northern France, the 16th (Irish) Division of the British Army sustained one of the heaviest gas attacks of the war. Clouds of chlorine gas enveloped the Irish trenches.

A chaplain with the Royal Dublin Fusiliers wrote to his father, 'There they lay, scores of them (we lost 800, nearly all from gas) in the bottom of the trench, in every conceivable posture of human agony; the clothes torn off their bodies in a vain effort to breathe while from end to end of that valley of death came one long unceasing moan from the lips of brave men fighting and struggling for life.'

The gas, according to one veteran, 'produces a flooding of the lungs – it is an equivalent death to drowning only on dry land. The effects are these – a splitting headache and terrific thirst (to drink water is instant death), a knife edge of pain in the lungs and the coughing up of a greenish froth off the stomach and the lungs, ending finally in insensibility and death. The colour of the skin from white turns a greenish black and yellow, the colour protrudes and the eyes assume a glassy stare. It is a fiendish death to die.'

Among the dead were Privates Joseph Pender and Paddy Byrne, both from Dublin. Both were aged just 17. In all, 538 men died and 1,590 were injured.

The number of deaths was significantly greater than that on all sides in the Easter Rising.

'Field kitchens had followed us up and gave what they could. I was just seeing to the company's rations when Capt. Cooper told me "Dick, get along and have some breakfast: that old boy has got some food in his house there."

'I said, "Isn't there anything I can do here, sir?" He snapped "Do what you're told", and as I did so he called after me, "That's a damn silly question, isn't it?"

'This kind old gentleman (the Irishman, I mean, not Cooper: they both were) had set his household frying rations galore for a first batch of us, with a second relay for Cooper and the others.'

Fighting was continuing across the city.

At the South Dublin Union, Eamonn Ceannt's 120-strong garrison came under renewed and fierce attack. Close quarters fighting had taken place within the corridors of a building that at the time held 3,200 staff and patients. As each side tunnelled their way through the complex, it had become a savage place. Nurses had spent the week attempting to protect and calm the terrified patients, many of whom were mentally ill, and one nurse, Margaretta Keogh, was accidentally shot by British troops when she appeared at an opening in one of the corridors.

Liam T. Cosgrave was among the band of rebels holding out. 'During the engagement the plaster was shot off the walls and ceilings. Holes were breached in the walls from one room to the next to permit more freedom of movement when the attack increased in severity. Explosions went on repeatedly and every now and then a shower of bricks would fall from the Nurses' Home.'

Tired and dispirited Volunteers, several of them having joined Ceannt in saying the Rosary in anticipation of a final assault, were revitalised by the actions of their vice-commandant, Cathal Brugha. In defending a barricade, he would suffer 25 wounds in all before finally being evacuated on the Friday.

Elsewhere, the surrender of the Mendicity Institute had left Ned Daly's Four Courts rebel garrison under siege by troops. The government sent improvised armoured vehicles – Guinness lorries covered with old boilers and iron plates – into the fray, but fighting along nearby North King Street was house to house.

Con O'Donovan's position in the Four Courts came under heavy fire. 'One man was with me at the loop-hole, on the lower of the two floors we occupied, while two others were

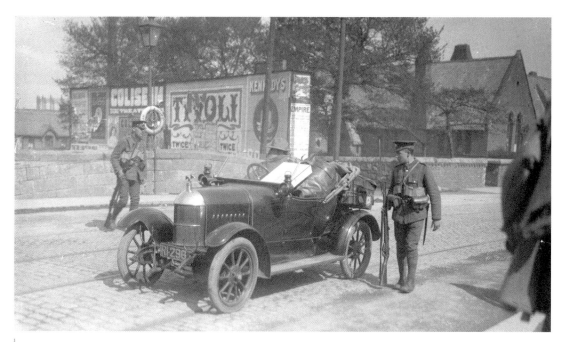

British troops search a car at Mount Street Bridge. As the week went on, it became increasingly difficult to get around the city, with the head of BP in Ireland, Ernest Jordison, cycling from Clontarf to Drogheda to bring his children to safety.

similarly posted on the floor above. The big gun appeared on the south side of the Liffey, in that inset in the Quay, close to St Michael and John's Church. We kept peppering away at the gunners whenever one of them showed himself but, as we did not get much chance of taking deliberate aim, I cannot say that we hurt any of them. Perhaps we did.

'Then came a shattering explosion, and the room trembled. Their first shell hit rather low, between the two windows of the room I was in. We had not enough sense, or military training, to then retreat, but kept on having a shot at the gunners. Soon, the second shell entered our room, through the window at which we were not. Why they put it through that window, in preference to the one at which two of us were stationed, which was nearer to them and to the corner of the building, I could not explain.

'For more than a minute after that shell burst in the room, I think we did not realise whether we were dead or alive. I remember distinctly, while the room was full of dust, smoke and falling ceiling, hearing the voice of a comrade from the floor above, calling my name and asking were we dead or alive down there.

Con Colbert, who gave lessons in how to make crude pikes to the rebels at Marrowbone Lane distillery. Colbert would be among those executed for his part in the Rising.

'The humour of that question aroused me, and I then realised that my comrade and myself were uninjured. I called to the man above to come down quickly and follow me, as I realised that the next shell would probably enter the room they were in, directly above us. We made our way to the ground floor where we found our comrades praying for us, as dead.'

For Robert Holland and the garrison at Marrowbone Lane, dawn on Thursday had brought the sight of British soldiers surrounding the distillery. 'Trenches had been dug on both sides of the Canal, also the Fairbrother's Field and we settled down for a "battle royal". All rifles are brought into play and Jack Saul, my brother Dan, Mick White and myself took up positions facing four different directions. At the usual time the girls brought along our breakfast, tea and bread. I did not know what had happened the beast that I had killed the day before as we got no meat. The girls kept loading the rifles and we were allocated three rifles each. I occasionally used one of the Howth guns and was driven about 12ft across the floor every time I fired it.'

At about 2pm, with soldiers reaching the outer boundaries of the distillery, Holland and four other Volunteers were brought to the yard and given hand grenades. In the Main Hall, Con Colbert was giving lessons on how to use them, and also on how to use crude pikes being made on the premises. Holland describes these weapons. 'They were being made out of scrap iron picked up around the Brewery Yard and put on what looked like broken broom handles. They only consisted of a piece of steel with a sharp point and I began wishing that I had taken the soldiers' bayonets as well as the ammunition.

'Frank Saul then heard some talking outside the Canal gate where he was at the time and he and someone else threw one of the grenades over the wall. We heard some screeching and shouting outside and a lot of moaning. As a result, the soldiers at the outside of the wall ran away from it and they were fired on by a volley from the Distillery. I saw Con Colbert smile as he sent us back into the building again saying, "that stops the attack for the present". When I got up on top again, the soldiers had become scarce but I could see a lot of bodies all around outside the wall and up as far as Dolphin's Barn Bridge. I could just see a pit and Red Cross men working at it putting bodies into it at the Bridge.

'Other Red Cross men started to dig a pit in Fairbrother's Field and we stopped firing in that direction.'

James Stephens would recall another day of wild rumour, but there was no doubting the ferocity of some of the violence. 'At 11.30am there came the sound of heavy guns firing in the direction of Sackville Street. I went on the roof, and remained there for some time. From this height the sounds could be heard plainly. There was sustained firing along the whole central line of the City, from the Green down to Trinity College, and from thence to Sackville Street, and the report of the various types of arm could be easily distinguished. There were rifles, machine guns and very heavy cannon. There was another sound which I could not put a name to, something that coughed out over all the other sounds, a short, sharp bark, or rather a short noise something like the popping of a tremendous cork.'

For Mrs Hamilton Norway, the situation was causing particular problems. 'Yesterday, to our great indignation, the public-houses were allowed to be open from 2pm till 5pm, though every shop, bank, and public building was closed – just to inflame the mob, it could not have been on any other grounds; and yet at 8pm, after being on duty from 5am, H (her husband Arthur) could not get a whiskey and soda, or even a glass of cider with his dinner, as it was out of hours. I was furious!'

Until the afternoon, there had been a gun battle around Grafton Street, and when it was over the looters descended on the area, targeting a nearby fruit shop. 'From the windows we watched the proceedings, and I never saw anything so brazen!

'The mob were chiefly women and children with a sprinkling of men. They swarmed in and out of the side door bearing huge consignments of bananas, the great bunches on the stalk, to which children attached a cord and ran away dragging it along.

'It was an amazing sight and nothing daunted these people. Higher up at another shop we were told a woman was hanging out of a window and dropping down loot to a friend, when she was shot through the head by a sniper … the body dropped into the street and the mob cleared. In a few minutes, a hand-cart appeared and gathered up the body, and instantly all the mob swarmed back to continue the joyful proceedings!'

On the other hand, by Thursday, O'Connell Street was finally deserted of pedestrians.

In the GPO, according to Dick Humphreys, 'The everlasting wait for the unexpected is terribly nerve-wracking. Machine guns stutter irregularly from all sides and add to the growing uproar.'

There was rumour of an impending attack. 'The excitement grows intense. Everyone is waiting. Suddenly rumour has it that an armoured car is approaching up Henry Street. Men show themselves insanely at the window to obtain a view. Then comes a tremendous explosion rising high above the rattle of rifle and machine gun fire. The shooting dies down all at once, and there is a lull.'

At this point, just after 3pm, Pearse spoke to the men, telling them, among other things, that the country had risen, a large band of insurgents was making its way from Dundalk to Dublin and large numbers of police had been captured after a battle in the north Co. Dublin village of Lusk.

According to Dick Humphreys, 'His words are answered by a deafening outburst of cheering which spreads throughout the whole building. Needless to say, this account puts new vitality into the men which three days' uncertainty and suspense had rather dispersed.'

Shortly after his speech, the shelling of the area intensified, while the building began to take fire from two howitzer guns mounted near Findlater's Church on Parnell Square. 'For 10 or 15 minutes our roof-snipers stand the fire, but begin to suffer heavily, three wounded severely. Word to evacuate this position is accordingly given, and a minute later they come tumbling through the main safety man-holes into the telegraph room. Some of the men in their hurry fail to catch the rope altogether and take a drop of 18 feet as though it was an everyday occurrence.

'The wounded are lowered safely by means of two ropes. This cannonade continues for about two and half hours, but the shells, the majority of which seem to be shrapnel, fail to do any serious damage to our position.'

A curious O'Connell Street crowd looks at a railway boiler, converted into an armoured car by the British Army. Guinness trucks were also made into makeshift armoured vehicles.

However, during that afternoon, James Connolly – who had been a calm and ubiquitous figure in the GPO and around O'Connell Street all week – was wounded when a ricochet caught him as he stepped from Middle Abbey Street to urge on a party of Volunteers. The bullet caused a compound fracture of his left shinbone, crippling him and leaving him confined to a stretcher on the floor.

Meanwhile, flames began to engulf the street, watched by Oscar Traynor from the Metropole Hotel. 'Some time on Thursday a barricade which stretched from the Royal

A view of the damage along O'Connell Street.

SPORTS EXTRA!

In the 1916 All-Ireland football final, Wexford beat Mayo 3-4 to 1-2. In the hurling final, Tipperary (represented by Boherlahan) beat Kilkenny (Tullaroan) 5-4 to 3-2. Famously, Croke Park's Hill 16 was originally made from the rubble of O'Connell Street, although then it was a grassy hill rather than a stepped terrace. Included among the material was the mangled remains of The O'Rahilly's car.

A view of the destruction as seen from Henry Street. Nelson's Pillar appears to rise from the rubble.

Hibernian Academy to a cycle shop – I think the name of it was Keating's – on the opposite side of the street, took fire as a result of a direct shell hit. It was the firing of this barricade that caused the fire that wiped out the east side of O'Connell Street. I saw that happen myself. I saw the barricade being hit; I saw the fire consuming it and I saw Keating's going up. Then Hoyt's caught fire, and when Hoyt's caught fire the whole block up to Earl Street became involved.

'Hoyt's had a lot of turpentine and other inflammable stuff, and I saw the fire spread from there to Clery's. Clery's and the Imperial Hotel were one and the same building ...

'Before that happened those of us in the Metropole made tremendous efforts to warn the garrison in the Imperial Hotel of the grave danger which menaced them. If our messages, which were sent by semaphore, were understood they do not appear to have been acted on, as the eventual evacuation of the Imperial Hotel appears to have been a rather hurried one.

'I had the extraordinary experience of seeing the huge plate-glass windows of Clery's stores run molten into the channel from the terrific heat.'

As they fled the flames of the Imperial Hotel, fighters improvised a most basic type of bullet-proof vest by wrapping themselves in large mattresses before running across the street.

As government troops approached from the direction of the Abbey Theatre, the firing was so continuous that the rebels' weapons became overheated. Without any suitable oil to cool them down, they improvised and used oil from sardine cans.

Things became so confused that when some horses bolted from a burning building, the rebels began shooting and throwing home-made bombs at them believing it to be a British cavalry charge.

'One of our men was swinging a home-made bomb, which was, in fact, a billy-can packed with bolts, nuts and, I believe, gelignite as the explosive,' recounted Traynor. 'He was swinging this bomb around his head in order to gain impetus for his throw when, to our horror, the handle parted company with the can and the can flew into the room instead of being thrown at the horses. Luckily for us it did not explode. I think three bombs, none of which exploded, were thrown.'

Things were far quieter out of the city. Ernest Jordison, head of British Petroleum in Ireland, had spent the day taking his children to the safety of Drogheda, where he left three of his children with a cousin of his wife. They had cycled all the way from Clontarf, on Dublin's north side. 'I returned home from Drogheda after leaving my children there, and took my children's bicycle along with me, pushing it along while riding my own. I had a few minutes' stay in Balbriggan for refreshment, and continued my journey to Clontarf without incident.

'After leaving the main road at Santry, along the lanes, cycling through Coolock and Killester, everything was still and quiet except for the corncrakes craking, the weather was very beautiful and fine, and the country was lighted up from the reflection in the skies of the fires in Dublin city. I hardly met a soul the whole way home from Balbriggan. I could hear the guns being fired in the city, and the flames and reflections were very vivid over the city.'

As night fell, the planet Venus shone brilliantly, but the sky glowed red. Across the city, Dubliners could see their city burning.

'This night also was calm and beautiful, but this night was the most sinister and woeful of those that have passed,' wrote James Stephens. 'The sound of artillery, of rifles, machine guns, grenades, did not cease even for a moment. From my window I saw a red flare that crept to the sky, and stole over it and remained there glaring; the smoke reached from the ground to the clouds, and I could see great red sparks go soaring to enormous heights; while always, in the calm air, hour after hour there was the buzzing and rattling and thudding of guns, and, but for the guns, silence.'

Mary Louisa Hamilton Norway watched the fires from her window on Dawson Street. 'It was the most awe-inspiring sight I have ever seen. It seemed as if the whole city was on fire, the glow extending right above the heavens and the red glare hundreds of feet high, while above the roar of the fires the whole air seemed to be vibrating with the noise of the great guns and machine-guns. It was an inferno!'

LEADERS FLEE THE GPO AS REBELLION NEARS END

Friday, April 28th

- GENERAL MAXWELL ARRIVES IN THE EARLY HOURS, AND ISSUES A PROCLAMATION.

- SIGNIFICANT REBEL ASSAULT ON ASHBOURNE, CO. MEATH TAKES MORE THAN 90 PRISONERS AND CAPTURES FOUR POLICE BARRACKS.

- DECISION TAKEN AT 8PM TO EVACUATE THE BURNING GPO.

- PEARSE, CONNOLLY, PLUNKETT, CLARKE AND MACDERMOTT HALT IN A HOUSE ON MOORE STREET, WHERE THEY PLAN TO MAKE THEIR WAY THROUGH BACK STREETS TO THE FOUR COURTS FOR A LAST STAND.

- GOVERNMENT TROOPS ON NORTH KING STREET KILL MORE THAN A DOZEN INNOCENT CIVILIANS.

- ON THE EASTERN FRONT, THE GERMANS ROLL BACK PREVIOUS GAINS MADE THE PREVIOUS MONTH BY A RUSSIAN ADVANCE AT LAKE NAROCH, LITHUANIA.

As Friday morning broke, from his position in the GPO, Dick Humphreys surveyed the scene. 'The weather is sunny and fine as usual. On the opposite side of O'Connell Street nothing is left of the buildings save the bare walls. Clouds of grey smoke are wreathing around everywhere, and it is difficult to see as far as the Bridge. Occasionally some side wall or roof falls in with a terrific crash. The heat is stupefying, and a heavy odour of burning cloth permeates the air. All the barbaric splendour that night had lent the scene has now faded away, and the pitiless sun illuminates the squalidness and horror of the destruction.'

This depiction of the scene in the GPO during the latter part of Easter Week shows the building in flames and a wounded James Connolly confined to a stretcher on the floor.

In the early hours of Friday morning, General Sir John Grenfell Maxwell had finally arrived in Dublin as commander-in-chief of the forces in Ireland. He issued a proclamation:

'The most vigorous measures will be taken by me to stop the loss of life and damage to property which certain misguided persons are causing in their armed resistance to the law. If necessary I shall not hesitate to destroy any buildings within any area occupied by the rebels and I warn all persons within the area specified below, and now surrounded by HM troops, forthwith to leave such area.'

The Sherwood Foresters had spent the night in the quadrangle of Kilmainham Hospital, and Capt. Dickson remembers that they 'were paraded for congratulations by Gen. Sir John Maxwell on our work – our first active service – in the difficult job of street fighting'. After which, Capt. Dickson used his first free time to write to the family of his friend Hawken, who had been killed at Mount Street. He thought of his dead friend, and another who was severely wounded, and was thankful that 'all I got was the bullet lodged in my Pocket Book.'

SUNDAY
23
MONDAY
24
TUESDAY
25
WEDNESDAY
26
THURSDAY
27
FRIDAY
28
SATURDAY
29

Not all the soldiers were engaged in such a noble task. Patrick Bermingham of the Dublin Metropolitan Police was at St Patrick's Close beside the cathedral when he saw a government soldier 'very much intoxicated, firing indiscriminately in the air and at windows and doors. Then he would lay down his rifle and light his cigarette and then carry on firing as before ... We arrested him.'

For Dubliners, both news and supplies were low. 'This morning there are no newspapers, no bread, no milk, no news,' James Stephens wrote. 'The sun is shining, and the streets are lively but discreet. All people continue to talk to one another without distinction of class, but nobody knows what any person thinks.

'Guns do not sound so bad in the day as they do at night, and no person can feel lonely while the sun shines ...

'From the roof there comes the sound of machine guns. Looking towards Sackville Street one picks out easily Nelson's Pillar, which towers slenderly over all the buildings of the neighbourhood. It is wreathed in smoke.

'In many parts of the city hunger began to be troublesome. A girl told me that her family, and another that had taken refuge with them, had eaten nothing for three days. On this day her father managed to get two loaves of bread somewhere, and he brought these home. "When", said the girl, "my father came in with the bread the whole 14 of us ran at him, and in a minute we were all ashamed for the loaves were gone to the last crumb, and we were all as hungry as we had been before he came in." "The poor man", said she, "did not even get a bit for himself."'

At The Royal Hibernian Hotel, Mary Louisa Hamilton Norway met a fellow guest. 'A very delicate elderly lady who is staying here said to me this morning, in answer to inquiry as to how she had slept: "I could not sleep at all. When the guns ceased the awful silence made me so nervous!" I know exactly what she meant. When the roar of the guns ceases you can feel the silence.'

Victory for the government forces, she felt, was inevitable, but not imminent. 'We now have 30,000 troops and plenty of artillery and machine-guns, so the result cannot be uncertain, though there is desperate work to be done before the end is in sight.'

Without any hard news, John Joly found the rumour mill infuriating. 'A feature of these curious times was the prevalence of extraordinary rumours as to what was going on in the

'I HAD EIGHT DEAD MEN IN THE CART WHEN I HAD FINISHED'

Outside Dublin, the major engagement of the Easter Rising took place in Ashbourne, Co. Meath. It was carried out by the Fingal Battalion (based in north Co. Dublin), only half of whom – about 60 men – mobilised on Easter Monday. Led by Thomas Ashe, they began the week as disorganised and inexperienced, with only a few rifles and limited ammunition. Their chief advantage, it seemed, was that each rebel brought a bicycle, giving them some mobility.

Once the Rising began, the battalion's orders were to take the main road at Finglas and ambush army officers returning from the Fairyhouse races. No officers came their way. They was also instructed to blow up a railway bridge over Rogerstown Estuary, in north Co. Dublin, in order to disrupt military communications, but an attempt to do this caused only minor damage when the current proved too strong for the explosives to be placed around its pillars.

Then, on the Tuesday, Patrick Pearse requested that Ashe send 40 of his small battalion men to the GPO. He sent 20. A few stray rebels did add to his dwindling band, most notably Richard Mulcahy, an Irish Volunteer officer and IRB member who would later become IRA chief of staff and then commander of the Free State Army. Having started out the Rising on a fruitless sabotage mission at Howth Junction, his joining up with the Fingal Battalion proved to be an organisational boon.

As the week progressed, the Fingal Battalion expected to be joined by others from nearby Skerries, and to join up with those from counties Meath and Louth. It never happened, but the small battalion became more organised and efficient as it split into four fighting columns – an early example of the guerrilla tactics that would prove so valuable to the IRA in future years. One column would stay and protect the camp, while the others would go on raids. Ashe sent three columns on a successful raid of the post office and RIC barracks in Swords. Weapons and a small amount of ammunition were taken, and a bread van was commandeered. Its driver, in fact, stayed with the battalion for the remainder of the week at a reward of 10 shillings.

There were further raids on the RIC in the Dublin villages of Donabate and Garristown, where they also raided a post office and stole some money.

Just after 10.30am on Friday morning, the RIC barracks about half a mile north of Ashbourne was stormed by the insurgents. They had stopped off while on their way to destroy a nearby railway line. Ashe had offered the 40-strong police force a chance to surrender, sending two RIC officers captured on the journey to Ashbourne to deliver the message.

A post office worker, John Austen, was among those watching as Ashe and his men arrived on their bicycles, with rifles slung over their shoulders. 'The police refused to surrender. Ashe went back to his men, got them under cover and the battle began in earnest.

SUNDAY
23

MONDAY
24

TUESDAY
25

WEDNESDAY
26

THURSDAY
27

FRIDAY
28

SATURDAY
29

'Some of the rebels got onto the footpath along the road, behind the fence in front of the barracks, and behind the fence on the opposite side of the road, whilst some others were on the north side of the barracks. Some were behind a wall which was on the south-west side of the crossroads.'

A gun battle began, with the rebels gaining the upper hand and about to force an RIC surrender, when a column of about 55 police in 17 cars suddenly arrived from the village of Slane. What's more, there was confusion among the Volunteers when an attack from north of their position, which at first indicated police reinforcements, was actually coming from one of their own columns. However, the insurgents managed to outflank the RIC force, whose commanding officer had been badly wounded early in the battle. Ashe's men eventually won out when Mulcahy led a charge with fixed bayonets, and the RIC officers surrendered. The police had suffered heavy casualties, with eight killed and 15 wounded. The rebels had one man killed and six wounded (one of whom would later die of those injuries).

Austen was asked to assist in moving the bodies. He used a horse and cart for the purpose. 'I told Ashe what I was going to do, and he told me to go ahead. Two of the policemen who had not been wounded helped me to collect the dead policemen into the cart. I had eight dead men in the cart when I had finished ... Two of the dead men were civilians who I believe were drivers of cars.'

The rebels, buoyed by their victory, made off to set up camp and await orders. When an order did come from Dublin, however, it told them to surrender.

British soldiers hold a Dublin street. For several days, the government forces struggled to contain the small force of rebels, with fierce fighting on Mount Street causing especially large casualties.

115

A British machine gun section in south Dublin during the rebellion. Machine gun positions were also in three positions across St Stephen's Green, and looking up O'Connell Street.

world outside. The tendency to imagine the worst was consistently manifested in these reports. Verdun had fallen; there had been a great naval battle disastrous to British supremacy; there had been a landing of Germans on the East Coast of England. With such items of news we were regaled, and on the most conclusive evidence.

'Nor were events nearer home more favourably reported. The number of risings in the Irish counties and the strength of the Rebels were alike exaggerated. All this did not conduce to our peace of mind. Fortunately the immediate surroundings were too engrossing to permit us to reflect on the calamities which appeared to be crowding upon Great Britain during our temporary sequestration from the newspapers.'

Joly heard salacious tales of the looting of the burning city. 'It was related that looting was going on, on a most disgraceful scale. Shops of all sorts were broken open and the goods freely distributed to the citizens of the Irish Republic.

'Men stripped off their old clothes and dressed themselves anew in the open streets, donning fashionable suits. Women selected jewels for their personal adornment, and rich and rare were the gems they wore on toil-stained fingers and grimy wrist. Watches were carried off heaped in aprons. Toys were given to the young. Fruit and champagne and other expensive luxuries were freely partaken of. The wines were in some cases retailed for a few pence the bottle. Bookshops only were immune from attack. It is related that some officers captured by the Rebels on Monday were conveyed by the enemy to a tobacconist's shop, and with true Irish hospitality were treated to the best cigars, the owner of the shop having fled.'

In Marrowbone Lane distillery, 19-year-old insurgent Robert Holland was in better mood. 'Throughout the night we all slept in our turn for a few hours although it seemed that we only closed our eyes. All during the night the firing and banging continued and still our dogged spirit is 100 per cent with us all. We are winning and nothing else matters. We will surely get that help. The Germans could not be far from Dublin now and the country Volunteers are showing the way.'

Nonetheless, that morning, 'we thought the city must all be on fire as we saw the big red glow through clouds of smoke'. Shooting was sporadic. For the second time that week, this apprentice butcher was asked to kill a cow, and once again was not given any of the meat. 'I asked for some. I was told it was Friday and handed a can of soup and some bread.'

'VERY OFTEN THE INNOCENT SUFFER FOR THE GUILTY'

During Friday night and Saturday morning, government troops killed a number of men and boys on North King Street, near the Four Courts. Kate Kelly, a domestic servant, was present at the deaths of Thomas Hickey (38), his son Christopher Hickey (16) and a neighbour, Peter Connolly (39), who had been discussing the moving of two mirrors of Hickey's when the military rushed down the street and left him unable to return home.

'About 6am on Saturday morning I heard a noise of picking at the walls. I shouted at Mr Hickey, "Someone is breaking into the house." He got up, and soon after, several soldiers dashed through a hole which they had made in the wall from next door ... the soldiers had drawn bayonets and crowbars and picks.'

The four were taken prisoner, even though they insisted they were not insurgents. 'I remember well, the bell was ringing for 10 o'clock Mass. We were then led in through the hole in the wall through the rooms of Mrs Carroll next door ...

'The officer said, "March on, the female first." Mr and Mrs Carroll and her daughter were in their room, and as they knew their neighbour, Mr Hickey, well, they spoke to him. Mr Hickey, as he passed, said to Mrs Carroll, "Isn't it too bad, Mrs Carroll?" "Yes indeed, Mr Hickey," she said, and the last thing he said to her was, "Very often the innocent suffer for the guilty."

'As I came to the hole in the wall I stumbled, was frightened, and nearly fell down. I fell down on the floor of the empty house when I got inside and called out, "I hope they are not going to kill us." The soldier replied with a laugh, "You are a bally woman, you're all right." I was left lying in the front room and the men were brought into the back.

'Both Mrs Carroll and I heard poor Christy pleading for his father's life – "Oh! Don't kill father." The shots then rung out, and I shouted, "Oh my God!" and overcome with horror, I threw myself on my knees and began to pray.'

Jacob's Biscuit Factory around the time of the Rising. Its garrison of rebels was led by Thomas MacDonagh, a signatory of the Proclamation, however it had little influence on the overall battle.

GUESTS OF THE REBELLION

During Easter week, the Gaiety Theatre was to stage the operas of Gilbert and Sullivan, performed by a travelling company called D'Oyly Carte. It was cancelled, and an account of a week spent in Dublin during the rebellion came from the actor Henry Lytton, who was staying for the week at the Gresham Hotel on O'Connell Street. 'The very first day we were not allowed out at all, for we were in the very centre of hostilities, and no one could go into the street except at his peril. Chafing under the restraint, I did at last attempt to venture out, though feeling that there were too many bullets about for things to be healthy ...

'Conditions in the hotel itself were the reverse of pleasant, what with the noise of the firing outside and bullets shooting through our own windows, though these were shuttered and protected as far as possible. Our food stocks commenced to run low – by the end of the week's siege we had only biscuits and ham – and the strain on the larder was added to by the arrival of scores of visitors who had been turned out of the Metropole Hotel.

In good spirits, the rebels believed they would be there for some time. 'There was no mention of any of us surrendering at any time.' In fact, plans were made for a céilí. 'I sent down one of the girls to ask permission to go down to the Main Hall. I went down. This was about 10pm and the usual Rosary had been started. When this had finished, we had a talk with some of the girls as we all knew one another. During this chat some of the girls suggested that we should get some kind of music and have a céilídhe for Sunday night. Alice Corcoran said she would try and get her brother's violin if any of the Fianna boys would go for it.

'The main hall was lighted up with candles but no light was visible from outside. When I got back to my post the city looked like an inferno; every place seemed to be burning and there was the usual firing and heavy explosions.'

On O'Connell Street the shells – many of them incendiary shells – were having their effect.

At 9.30am Patrick Pearse wrote a manifesto – on official government paper embossed with the Royal Arms – which admitted that the GPO was now isolated and its defenders were preparing for a final stand. He praised his men.

'Let me, who have led them into this, speak in my own, and in my fellow commanders' names, and in the name of Ireland present and to come, their praise, and ask those who come after them to remember them.

'For four days, they have fought and toiled, almost without cessation, almost without sleep, and in the intervals of fighting, they have sung the songs of the freedom of Ireland. No man has complained, no man has asked "why?" Each individual has spent himself, happy to pour out his strength, for Ireland and for freedom. If they do not win this fight, they will at least have deserved to win it. But win it they will, although they may win it in death.'

Pearse took his opportunity to comment on Eoin MacNeill's countermanding order. 'If we accomplish no more than we have accomplished, I am satisfied. I am satisfied that we have saved Ireland's honour. I am satisfied that we should have accomplished more, that we should have accomplished the task of enthroning, as well as proclaiming, the Irish Republic as a Sovereign State, had our arrangements for a simultaneous rising of the whole country, with a combined plan as sound as the Dublin plan has been proved to be, been allowed to go through on Easter Sunday. Of the fatal countermanding order which prevented those plans from being carried out, I shall speak no further. Both Eoin MacNeill and we have acted in the best interests of Ireland.'

Of James Connolly, Pearse wrote, 'He lies wounded, but is still the guiding brain of our resistance'.

Connolly was badly wounded and now propped on an iron bed, but he still took a chance to dictate a separate, somewhat more optimistic, pronouncement. Among his claims were that 'the men of North County Dublin are in the field, have occupied all the Police barracks in the district, destroyed all the telegram system on the Great Northern Railway up to Dundalk, and are operating against the trains of the Midland and Great Western.

'Dundalk has sent 200 men to march upon Dublin, and in the other parts of the North our forces are active and growing.'

Galway was rising, he continued. Wexford and Wicklow are strong. Cork and Kerry 'are equally acquitting themselves creditably'. The rebels' German allies and kinsmen in America were 'straining every nerve to hasten matters on our behalf'.

He added: 'As you know, I was wounded twice yesterday, and am unable to move about, but have got my bed moved into the firing line, and with the assistance of your officers, will be just as useful to you as ever.

'They had been told to take their valuables with them, and it was remarkable how, in the fright of such an emergency, men would grasp the first thing that came into their hands and leave their real treasures behind. One man rushed over clutching two dirty collars, while another had a bath-towel which he had picked up, it seemed, instead of a dressing-gown. English jockeys who were there for the race week hurried over holding a saddle case.'

The rebels were forced to evacuate the GPO on the evening of Friday, April 28th after fierce shelling wrought great damage. Here, British soldiers inspect the interior of the almost completely destroyed building.

'Courage, boys, we are winning, and in the hour of our victory, let us not forget the splendid women who have everywhere stood by us and cheered us on. Never had a man or woman a grander cause, never was a cause more grandly served.'

Oscar Traynor was still leading the garrison in the Metropole Hotel, which was now on fire. They held out for most of the day until receiving an order to return to the GPO.

'When we arrived at the post office, Pearse sent for me and asked me why did we evacuate our post. I informed him that my second-in-command had received a message from some person in the GPO. When we tried to confirm that fact we failed. I immediately saw that some mistake had been made, and I suggested to Commandant Pearse that we should return ... we returned immediately and re-occupied all our former positions.'

In the GPO, the first direct hit from a shell came at 3pm, and others soon followed. Eamon Bulfin recalled: 'I remember distinctly the Post Office being hit by shells. We were informed that the floor above us was made of ferroconcrete and that there was absolutely no danger of the floor coming down.'

'At first the hoses were working perfectly but, after a while, apparently the water was cut off or the mains failed. There was no water at all.'

A view of O'Connell Street showing the extensive damage done by a combination of fires and shelling by the gunboat Helga, *which had sailed up the Liffey.*

A COLOURFUL VIEW FROM GERMANY

On April 28th, as word of the Rising spread to Germany, a writer in the *Vossische Zeitung* newspaper wrote a rather disparaging article about the English, headlined 'England's Guilt Towards Ireland':

'... the English soul is so easily understood, especially in his reaction to parts of the empire! The example of the travelling Englishman in the train compartment shows it in a nutshell. He will put his legs on your lap in order to go to sleep. You will complain – he only smiles mockingly. He knows that complaining hasn't much value, that complaining is a poor substitute for action. He is also able to complain but then you coolly take a piece of luggage, and, smiling in a friendly fashion, you put it on his shin bone. His legs will be retracted quickly: the whole man wants to jump. He looks at you furiously for a moment, and then himself smiles in a friendly fashion. Only a further five minutes, and you will be the best friends in the world. You are superior to him; he has seen that you are a man of deeds and strong enough to act against him. Then he would rather be agreeable instead of passing out his usual kick – against those who are weak. This is the policy in the empire, wherever Mr Englishman is opposed by a foreign people.'

The situation had become desperate.

'It was duskish on Friday night when we were all ordered into the main hall,' according to Bulfin's account. 'When we had assembled there we were addressed by Pearse. I don't remember his exact words. We were ordered to take as much food and ammunition as possible with us, and to try and get in – as far as I can remember now – to Williams and Woods factory [on Parnell Street]. I did not know where it was at the time. We got an order to unload weapons, and a chap standing beside me was wounded in the foot when his shotgun went off while in the process of being unloaded.'

It was 8pm, and the evacuation of the GPO had been ordered.

'We left the GPO and crossed Henry Street, under fire, into Henry Place. At the junction of Henry Place and Moore Lane, there was a house which we called the "White House". It was a small one-storied slated house as far as I remember, and was being hit by machine gun fire and rifle fire from the top of Moore Lane. We thought that fire was actually coming from the White House. Volunteers, with bayonets, were called on to charge this house and occupy it. It was very duskish, and we could not see very well. There was no cohesion. Nobody seemed to be in charge once we left the post office; it was every man for himself.'

A nurse, Elizabeth O'Farrell, had been one of only three women (all members of Cumann na mBan) left in the GPO after Pearse had ordered the others to leave that morning. 'We left in three sections, I being in the last. Commandant Pearse was the last to leave the building. He went round to see that no one was left behind. We immediately preceded him, bullets raining from all quarters as we rushed to Moore Lane.

'As I passed the barricade I tripped and fell; in a second a man rushed out of the house on the corner of Moore Lane and Moore Street, where the second section had taken cover, took me up in his arms and rushed back to the house.'

The Rising caused great problems for ordinary Dubliners, who struggled to get to work, to find food and, as obvious by this queue at the Dublin Savings Bank, to access their savings.

Having received the order to evacuate, Oscar Traynor had joined this party that included Bulfin. 'On entering one of the buildings in the middle of Moore Street we were met by a little family – an old man, a young woman and her children – cowering into the corner of a room, apparently terrified. I tried to reassure these people that they were safe. The old man stated that he was very anxious to secure the safety of his daughter and grandchildren, and that, for that reason, he intended to make an effort to secure other accommodation.

Ned Daly, who led the Four Courts garrison in close quarters fighting with the British. With the battle raging, the adjoining area of North King Street saw a massacre of civilians by British troops.

'It was his intention to leave the house under a flag of truce, which, he said, he felt sure would be respected. I did my best to dissuade him from taking this action, especially during hours of darkness. He, however, appeared to be very confident and said he would make the effort.

'I appealed to his daughter not to allow her father to take this action. It appears that he eventually ignored the advice which I gave him, because when we were forming up in Moore Street, preparatory to the surrender, I saw the old man's body lying on the side of the street almost wrapped in a white sheet, which he was apparently using as a flag of truce.'

Alongside Pearse and Connolly, the other leaders to escape from the GPO were Joseph Plunkett, Thomas Clarke and Seán MacDermott. They planned to make their way through the streets to the Four Courts garrison for a final battle. Nurse O'Farrell tended to Connolly. 'When I entered the parlour of the house I found some of the members of the provisional government already there, the house well barricaded, and James Connolly lying on a stretcher in the middle of the room. I went over and asked him how he felt; he answered: "Bad", and remarked: "The soldier who wounded me did a good day's work for the British government."

'After a short time the other members of the provisional government came in. Some mattresses were then procured, on which we placed Mr Connolly, and the other wounded men. There were 17 wounded in the retreat from the GPO and I spent the night helping to nurse them. Around us we could hear the roar of burning buildings, machine guns played on teahouses and at intervals what seemed to be hand grenades.'

Moving down the street, the rebels occupied buildings, punching their way through the walls. During the evening, The O'Rahilly had led a doomed charge down Henry Street, with most of those men, including himself, wounded or killed.

Elsewhere, Ned Daly's garrison was faring badly. The remaining fighters on North King Street numbered no more than seven or eight, and were cut off from Daly, who had pulled his headquarters back to the Four Courts. Days of fighting had driven one rebel mad, and he had to be handcuffed to a bed.

Escaping down the adjacent Church Street would be extremely difficult, and it was here that the fighting now concentrated. However, it would be a particularly bloody night for the civilians of North King Street. Between the Friday evening and Saturday morning, soldiers of the South Staffordshire Regiment killed more than a dozen innocent men.

The Rising was coming towards an end, although the people of Dublin were as yet unaware of this. 'It is hard to get to bed these nights,' wrote James Stephens. 'It is hard even to sit down, for the moment one does sit down one stands immediately up again, resuming that ridiculous ship's march from the window to the wall and back.

'I am foot weary as I have never been before in my life, but I cannot say that I am excited. No person in Dublin is excited, but there exists a state of tension and expectancy which is mentally more exasperating than any excitement could be. The absence of news is largely responsible for this. We do not know what has happened, what is happening, or what is going to happen, and the reversion to barbarism (for barbarism is largely a lack of news) disturbs us.

'Each night we have got to bed at last, murmuring, "I wonder will it be all over to-morrow", and this night the like question accompanied us.'

AND THEN IT WAS ALL OVER

Saturday, April 29th

- At noon, Pearse decides on ceasefire.

- At 12.45pm, nurse Elizabeth O'Farrell walks with a white flag towards the British.

- The rebels are offered only unconditional surrender.

- At 2.30pm Pearse surrenders, and after the garrison says the rosary it leaves 16 Moore Street.

- At 3.45pm Pearse is taken before General Maxwell at the headquarters of the Irish Command at Parkgate Street and signs a general order of surrender.

- Connolly countersigns the surrender order, but only for men under his command in Moore Street and St Stephen's Green.

- Ned Daly is allowed to lead a march of his men from the Four Courts to the surrender point at the Gresham Hotel.

- The rebels who surrender are corralled on open ground behind the Rotunda, where they remain for the night.

- On Sunday, garrisons at Boland's mill, Jacob's factory, St Stephen's Green, South Dublin Union and Marrowbone Lane surrender.

- The rebels are abused by angry Dubliners.

- The prisoners are marched to Richmond Barracks, where their leaders are identified.

- A 143-day siege of Kut in Iraq ends when the British General Charles Townshend surrenders to the Turks. Nine thousand British and Indians are taken prisoner. It is widely seen as the greatest single disaster in British military history.

On the Saturday morning, the sun shone once again. At 10am, Mary Louisa Hamilton Norway wrote a letter. 'If the main walls of the GPO remain standing it may be we shall find the safe in H's (her husband's) room still intact. It was built into the wall, and my jewel-case was in it, but all our silver, old engravings, and other valuables were stored in the great mahogany cupboards when we gave up our house in the autumn, as being the safest place in Dublin.'

The GPO was burnt out and empty, with its former occupiers continuing to burrow their way up the street. Among them was Joseph Sweeney, who was involved in a terrible incident on Moore Street. 'The door of the house we were trying to get into was locked and we could hear people moving about inside. We asked them to open the door and they wouldn't. Then somebody shouted in to get out of the room and he put a gun up to the door and blew open the lock. When we got in we found it had killed an old boy inside.'

A fishmonger's shop at number 16 Moore Street was chosen as the rebel headquarters and Sweeney was ordered to carry one end of James Connolly's stretcher. 'He had been shot above the ankle earlier in the week and the wound had become gangrenous. It was creeping up his leg by this time. And of course we had no supplies or dressings or any morphia to ease the pain, and he was in frightful agony. These houses were very small and the stairs very narrow and sometimes we had to lift the stretcher over the top and Connolly was roaring with the pain. It was pitiful to listen to him. Eventually we got him to a house that they had selected for a headquarters and I then moved further on towards the top of the street. By this time there was very little in the way of command. You simply moved with anybody you knew.'

In number 16, the leaders held a 'council of war'. Nurse Elizabeth O'Farrell was in the room at the time. 'On the floor of the room lay three wounded volunteers and a soldier, a prisoner who was badly injured, lay on a bed on the side of the room. Winifred Carney, Julia Grenan (the other Cumann na mBan members) and I came in to attend to them. The soldier asked us would Pearse speak to him. Pearse said "Certainly". The soldier then asked Pearse to lift him a little in the bed. Pearse did this, the soldier putting his arms around his neck. This was all. Pearse returned to James Connolly's bedside, and the consultation continued in private.'

Dublin in ruins in the aftermath of the rebellion. The shelling of the city centre caused a fire to engulf much of O'Connell Street and surrounding areas, with many buildings utterly destroyed.

It has been reported that, at around noon, Patrick Pearse witnessed something that convinced him to end the fight. Connolly told Dr James Ryan, who was in charge of the insurgents' medical unit, that Pearse was preparing to surrender. Out the window, Ryan saw a sight 'I shall never forget. Lying dead on the opposite footpath of Moore Street with white flags in their hands were three elderly men.' The men were dead, killed by machine-gun fire. 'Seán MacDermott came over to the window and pointed to the three dead men and said something like, "When Pearse saw that we decided we must surrender to save the lives of the citizens."'

At 12.45pm, Nurse O'Farrell was handed a hastily made Red Cross insignia and a white flag and asked to step outside and surrender to the troops.

'I waved the small white flag which I carried and the military ceased firing and called me up the barrier which was across the top of Moore Street into Parnell Street. As I passed up Moore Street I saw, at the corner of Sackville Lane, The O'Rahilly's hat and a revolver lying on the ground – I thought he had got into some house.

'I gave my message to the officer in charge, and he asked me how many girls were down there. I said three. He said: "Take my advice and go down again and bring the other two girls out of it." He was about putting me back again through the barrier when he changed his mind and said: "However, you had better wait, I suppose this will have to be reported."'

She met with a more senior officer.

O'Farrell told him, 'The commandant of the Irish Republican Army wishes to treat with the commandant of the British forces in Ireland.'

'The Irish Republican Army? – the Sinn Féiners, you mean,' he replied.

'No, the Irish Republican Army they call themselves and I think that is a very good name too.'

'Will Pearse be able to be moved on a stretcher?'

Patrick Pearse surrenders to General Lowe at the corner of Moore Street and Parnell Street at 2.30pm on Saturday. Lowe is accompanied by his son, while hidden from view behind Pearse is Nurse Elizabeth O'Farrell, who had conveyed messages between rebels and military.

'Commandant Pearse doesn't need a stretcher,' O'Farrell corrected him, at which point he turned to another officer and ordered, 'Take that Red Cross off her and bring her over there and search her – she's a spy.'

She was searched, finding, she would later recall, 'Two pairs of scissors (one of which he afterwards returned to me), some sweets, bread, and cakes, etc. Being satisfied that I wasn't dangerous he then took me (of all the places in the world) to Tom Clarke's shop as a prisoner.'

Brigadier General Lowe, who was in operational control of the government forces after General Maxwell's arrival, received word at the British headquarters in Park Gate Street. He jumped to his feet and, with his son (a lieutenant), and Kildare-man Captain Harry de Courcy-Wheeler, made his way towards Clarke's newsagent's shop.

'In peacetime the journey from Park Gate Street to our destination, the shop at the Parnell monument, would have been a matter of mere minutes,' recalled Wheeler. 'We took a zig-zag course in and out of side streets, taking the intervening corners at high speed to dodge the sharpshooters who were posted at vantage points on the roofs of the houses.

'Two bullets did get the panel of the near door of the car which was an official saloon supplied for use of the staff, owing to the skilful driver and the speed, I do not expect the snipers realised who were in it until it had skidded around the next corner.'

Lowe met with Nurse O'Farrell, and she was sent back to the rebels' position in Moore Street with a note and verbal message explaining to Pearse that there would be only an unconditional surrender. On her way, she saw a tragic sight. 'As I passed Sackville Lane, the first turn on the left in Moore Street going down from Parnell Street, I looked up and saw the dead body of The O'Rahilly lying about four yards up the lane – his feet against the steps of the first door on the right and his head on the curbstone.'

O'Farrell was set a deadline of half an hour. While Lowe waited for her he strolled onto O'Connell Street, in his full staff uniform. Wheeler realised that this would make him an attractive target for snipers. 'As the whole of Upper and Lower Sackville Street was held by rebels at this time, and I felt responsible for the general's safety, I pointed out that he would draw the fire on himself if spotted. He made little of it, but in the end I persuaded him to return to the newsagent's shop, and wait there for the dispatches from Commandant General Pearse.'

In order to prevent the further slaughter of Dublin
citizens, and in the hope of saving the lives of our
followers now surrounded and hopelessly outnumbered, the
members of the Provisional Government present at Head-
Quarters have agreed to an unconditional surrender, and the
Commandants of the various districts in the City and Country
will order their commands to lay down arms.

P. H. Pearse
29th April 1916
3.45 p.m.

I agree to these conditions for the men only
under my own Command in the Moore
Street District and for the men in
the Stephen's Green Command.

James Connolly
April 29/16

On consultation with Commandant Ceannt
and other officers I have decided to
agree to unconditional surrender also.

Thomas MacDonagh.

The Surrender of Headquarters.

Pearse's general order instructing the rebels to surrender, which was then countersigned by James Connolly,
although only for men 'under my own command'. Thomas MacDonagh followed in agreeing to 'unconditional
surrender'.

DAMAGE TO MORE THAN 200 BUILDINGS ESTIMATED AT £3M

The cost of the fire damage to buildings and stock in the city of Dublin was later estimated by the chief fire officer, Capt. Purcell, as £2.5 million. More than 200 buildings were damaged, he told the *Weekly Irish Times* on May 1st 1916. As his estimate of damages was based on rateable valuations, a figure of £3 million now looks more realistic.

Sackville Street, now O'Connell Street, was very badly hit. From Cathedral Street and Earl Street, an area fronted by Clery's department store was destroyed south to the Liffey. Hopkins and Hopkins, the jewellery shop on the corner of Eden Quay, was gone as was the entire series of blocks enclosed by Sackville Street to the west, and Marlborough Street to the north. This amounted to 27,000 square yards of prime city centre property.

Among the buildings damaged or destroyed were Clery's warehouse, the Royal Hibernian Academy, Wynn's Hotel, the Imperial Hotel, branches of the Munster and Leinster Bank and the Hibernian Bank. Public houses were hit, Nagle's and Sheridan's on North Earl Street and two branches of the famous Mooney's chain, one in Lower Abbey Street, the other on Eden Quay.

On the other side of the capital's wide main street, the devastation was as bad. Fire had raged from the GPO towards the Liffey, reaching back along Henry Street to Henry Place and Moore Street, advancing towards Liffey Street, almost as far as the Irish Independent's printing works on Middle Abbey Street. On the Sackville Street frontage, the Metropole Hotel, standing between Eason and the GPO, was gone, and with it adjoining buildings including the Oval Bar. Thom's Printing Works was destroyed.

The area affected by fire on this side of Sackville Street amounted to 34,000sq ft.

Outside the city centre, Capt. Purcell said his men had dealt with serious fires affecting two houses in Harcourt Street, and also at Ushers' Quay. There the fire had spread into Bridge Street, engulfing two tenement houses and Doherty's hotel, where it was halted just short of the city's oldest inn, the Brazen Head. His men had not been able to approach the Linen Hall Barracks, and the 32 clerks trapped there for four days during the Rising, had been forced to cope with two fires, the second started by bombs in a wooden structure to the rear.

The first call to the fire brigade came at 3.58pm on Monday, April 24th. It was from the ordnance department at Islandbridge, saying that there was a fire in the Magazine Fort in Phoenix Park which was used to store arms. The brigade found one section of the store on fire, containing large quantities of small arms and ammunition. They managed to save the remainder. Lieut John Myers (a great-uncle of the journalist Kevin Myers) of the fire brigade later denied that he was impeded in getting to the fire by armed Sinn Féiners.

What Capt. Purcell describes as the 'great fire' began in an auxiliary printing office owned by *The Irish Times* on Lower Abbey Street, backing on to Seville Place, at the side of Clery's on Thursday, April 27th. As the firing made

Dubliners stroll through the rubble and dust of O'Connell Street in the aftermath of Easter Week. It is now estimated that £3 million worth of damage was caused to Dublin city.

deployment too dangerous, 'All I could do was to observe through a glass from our tower [on Tara Street] the progress of the flames.'

From his vantage point, Capt. Purcell could see Clery's burning. 'I was hoping against hope it might withstand the fire but before morning it had gone the way of the rest.' And with went hopes that it might act as a fire break.

The ceasefire on Saturday meant that the firemen could work in comparative safety. Or so they thought. 'We were making excellent progress on both sides of Abbey Street when the bullets began to fly among us.' So the two motor tenders and the fire crews were withdrawn. The news came at 5.30pm that Nagle's public house in North Earl Street was burning furiously and Hickey's shop and Boyer's warehouse were at risk. Lieut John Myers and four men volunteered to tackle this outbreak. 'They ensured the safety of the remainder of the north side of Earl Street, including the cathedral at the back.'

But it wasn't over yet. At 8pm on Saturday, Capt. Purcell received many calls from doctors and clergymen at Jervis Street Hospital [on the site of the Jervis Centre]. Fires were spreading nearby and if they were not stopped, the patients would have to be moved. 'To the firemen's credit they one and all declared they would save the hospital, even under the bullets. We immediately hurried our available force out, recovered our engines and other apparatus from O'Connell Bridge and started out for the big fight,' said Capt. Purcell. He summoned help from fire crews at nearby Power's distillery and the Guinness brewery. 'We fought all during Saturday night, stopping the fire where it was possible … and saved the hospital.'

Though Pearse surrendered on Saturday, pockets of fighting continued, and most of the city remained a 'no-go area' for the brigade.

O'Farrell returned to the waiting General, and noticed his agitation. 'He was rather vexed because I was a minute over the half-hour coming, but I really wasn't, as I pointed out by my watch – then one of the officers set his watch by mine.'

At 2.30pm, General Lowe received Commandant Pearse at the top of Moore Street, in Parnell Street and accepted the rebels' unconditional surrender.

O'Farrell witnessed the moment. 'One of the officers that had been a prisoner in the GPO was asked to identify Pearse and he could not – he said he did not see him in the GPO. He asked Commandant Pearse was he in the GPO, and he said he was – the officer said: "I did not see you there." Commandant Pearse then handed his sword to General Lowe.'

SUNDAY
23

MONDAY
24

TUESDAY
25

WEDNESDAY
26

THURSDAY
27

FRIDAY
28

SATURDAY
29

Standing with them at this moment, Wheeler accepted some other items from Pearse. 'He handed over his arms and military equipment. His sword and automatic pistol in holster with pouch of ammunition, and his canteen, which contained two large onions, were handed to me by Commandant General Pearse. Onions were carried by insurgent troops as iron rations. They were believed to be high in nutriment value.'

Pearse was put in a car and taken to meet General Maxwell. As he was driven away a British officer commented, 'It would be interesting to know how many marks that fellow has in his pocket.'

At 3.45pm Pearse signed a general order instructing the rebels to surrender. Capt. de Courcy-Wheeler was instructed to take the order to James Connolly, who had been taken to a Red Cross hospital in Dublin Castle (he was so heavy it took seven men to carry him). Wheeler waited with him while his wounds were being dressed and then asked him if he was well enough to read and sign the order. Connolly said that he was, and then countersigned the order, but only for his Irish Citizen Army members in Moore Street and St Stephen's Green.

It was a surprise to many of the fighters. Oscar Traynor had earlier been told to prepare for a bayonet charge through Parnell Street. 'Almost on time for this charge to take place a volunteer rushed into this yard and said that the bayonet charge was to be cancelled. We did not know the reason for the cancellation, but, apparently, negotiations with the enemy were being considered. We were told to go to different rooms in the different houses and rest, and to be ready to carry on later in the evening, if necessary.

'I was terribly exhausted at this time and lay down. I apparently fell asleep, and remembered no more until I was awakened by some of my comrades who informed us that our garrison was surrendering. I naturally was astonished, as appeared to be most of my comrades.

'I remember, as we were going out onto Moore Street and crossing through the ruins of one of the house, meeting Seán MacDermott who was marshalling the men into the street, and I said to him: "Is this what we were brought out for? To go into English Dungeons for the rest of our lives?" Seán immediately waved a piece of paper which he held in his hand, and said: "No. We are surrendering as prisoners of war." This piece of paper, which he had in his hand, appeared to me to contain two signatures, but as I did not peruse the document I

As surrendered rebels were marched through the city, they were subjected to abuse from a public disgusted at the destruction of the city. 'This was the first time I ever appreciated the British troops as they undoubtedly saved us from being manhandled that evening,' recalled Robert Holland.

A REBEL PATCHWORK:
THE RISING OUTSIDE DUBLIN

There was confusion in the ranks of the Irish Volunteers around the country, following the countermanding order issued by Eoin MacNeill. The order was carried to a number of locations by The O'Rahilly who convinced leading Volunteers that it was genuine. Nonetheless, a number of units did make an attempt to join in the Rising.

GALWAY

In Co. Galway up to 1,000 Volunteers were mobilised, although the failure of the *Aud* meant that they carried a mixture of weapons that included pikes and pitchforks. They were led by Liam Mellows, a Volunteer who had been deported to England in 1915, but had returned via Belfast just in time for the Rising. He set up headquarters near Craughwell and from there launched attacks on a number of RIC barracks. Travelling by car, horse and cart and on horseback, the Volunteers arrived at Clarinbridge and Oranmore, stormed the police barracks and captured them. They were forced to retreat by the arrival of RIC reinforcements backed up by the military. In a separate incident in Carnmore an RIC constable was shot dead by a small party of rebels, reputedly as he shouted 'Surrender, boys, I know ye all.'

Mellows retreated to Athenry. He held most of his force together until it became clear that the Rising had failed in the rest of the country. On the Friday, 200 men decided to give up the fight and go home, after which the remaining men decided to break up. Mellows and some his fellow-leaders went into hiding. None of the rebels was killed in the fighting. One policemen died and three others were wounded.

WEXFORD

A force of 600 Volunteers led by Robert Brennan, Seamus Doyle and J.R. Etchingham seized control of Enniscorthy on Thursday of Easter week. Although the town was occupied after a surprise attack, the RIC barracks was held by a police inspector and five constables while an RIC sergeant and one constable prevented the rebels from taking over a bank in the town.

The Volunteers established a strong position on Vinegar Hill, overlooking the town. The railway line was cut and men dispatched to Gorey and Ferns. When about 50 men set off for Dublin they mistook a train carrying a few soldiers for an advanced government army and retreated. Before hostilities could develop the news of the Dublin surrender arrived, but the Volunteers refused to believe it. The army commander, Col F.A. French, was a Wexford man and in order to avoid bloodshed he offered a safe conduct for the Wexford leaders so that they could go to Dublin and hear of the surrender directly from Pearse. There were no fatalities.

CORK

The countermanding order caused confusion in Cork. Patrick Pearse sent a courier with a note saying 'We go into action at noon today', but that his orders were written on a page of a pocket diary undermined its authority. Although the Volunteers mobilised they did not proceed with the planned Rising as the government forces were alerted by the action in Dublin. After the intervention of the Catholic Bishop of Cork the Volunteers agreed to hand over their arms to the Lord Mayor for safe keeping. During a security operation after the Rising had ended, a part of the RIC surrounded a house at Castlelyons owned by the Kent family, who were prominent members of the Volunteers. A gun battle ensued in which Richard Kent and an RIC constable were killed and a number of policemen wounded. In the aftermath Thomas Kent was court-martialled and executed.

TIPPERARY

At Lisvernane, near Tipperary town, two policemen were shot dead attempting to arrest a Volunteer, Michael O'Callaghan. There was confusion among the Volunteers all week, with some of them, including Seán Treacy, urging action while others waited to see what would happen in Dublin. There was no general rising of Volunteers in the county.

LOUTH

As with so many other parts of the country, confusion was rife in Louth, with some believing that the Rising was off and others desperately trying to find out whether it was on or not. One Volunteer volunteered to cycle through a squally Sunday night to catch a Drogheda train to Dublin and find out what was going on. He arrived at Liberty Hall just as the rebels were about to leave for the GPO, and by the time he returned, the force of Volunteers had largely dissipated.

However, they then managed to force the surrender of several policemen and some British officers. At Castlebellingham they encountered a number of policemen and captured them, along with an army officer. In a confusing incident a Volunteer discharged a shot which wounded the officer and killed one of the policemen, Constable Charles McGee. As the force grew, James Connolly sent an order that it make its way to Dublin. However, the rebels then spent the rest of the week trying unsuccessfully to meet up first with Thomas Ashe's Fingal Battalion.

The rebel Thomas Ashe who led the only major battle to take place outside of Dublin. His small battalion caused heavy casualties on a raid on an RIC barracks in Ashbourne, Co. Meath.

143

cannot say what it contained. As we formed up on Moore Street the general discussion amongst the volunteers was that we were surrendering as prisoners of war and were being recognised as such by reason of having carried on the conflict over a certain period of time.'

Joseph Sweeney was among those who were now prisoners of war. 'We filed out onto Moore Street and were lined up into fours and were marched up O'Connell Street and formed into two lines on each side of the street. We marched up to the front and left all our arms and ammunition and then went back to our original places. Officers with notebooks then came along and took down our names. A funny incident happened there. One of the officers just looked at one of our fellows and without asking him anything wrote down his name and then walked on. After he had gone a certain distance, somebody asked this fellow, "Does that officer know you?" "That's my brother," he said.'

'We were ordered to dump as much stuff as we could in the houses,' according to Eamon Bulfin. 'We laid down arms between the Gresham and Parnell Monument. I don't remember any white flag. We were herded into the Rotunda Gardens, in a patch of grass in front. We were lying on top of one another. I was quite near Michael Collins and Joe Plunkett. I remember the British officer threatening to shoot the whole lot of us, and Collins saying to this officer, "This is a very sick man; will you leave him alone" – or words to that effect. He was, of course, referring to Joe Plunkett.'

Those identified as being under the age of 18 were sent home, as the young insurgent Seán Harling discovered. 'The officer who took the surrender seemed a very decent sort of fellow. I think he was a captain. I was just standing at the end of the line and he came along and he looks at me, you know, and he gives me a clip on the ear and tells me to get the hell home. I was very annoyed about not being arrested but that's what happened and I just watched the others being taken off as prisoners.'

Daniel O'Connell's statue stands untouched among the rubble of the street that would only later bear his name. Nevertheless, there are still bullet holes in his statue today caused by stray rounds during the Rising.

Constance Markievicz's surrender at the College of Surgeons, as depicted in a drawing by Grace Plunkett. Captain Harry de Courcy-Wheeler, who asked for her weapon, recalled: 'When handing over her arms she kissed her small revolver reverently.'

Nurse O'Farrell had been given surrender orders to be handed at the various posts. Accompanied by a priest, she went to meet Ned Daly at the Four Courts where he and his men reluctantly acceded.

As Joe Sweeney later recalled, 'During the night the garrison from the Four Courts came in and we were put lying on top of one another. I had two fellows lying on top of me. In one way it was desperate and in another way it was great, because it was a very cold night and they kept me warm.

'Anybody who put his foot out of line got a whack of a rifle butt. We were kept there all night and a British officer amused himself by taking out some of the leaders. He took out poor old Tom Clarke and, with the nurses looking out of the windows of the hospital, he stripped him to the buff and made all sorts of disparaging remarks about him. "This old bastard has been at it before. He has a shop across the street there. He's an old Fenian", and so on, and he took several others out too.

'That officer's name was Lee Wilson and I remember a few years later I happened to be in the bar of the Wicklow Hotel and Mick Collins in his usual way stomped in and said to me, "We got the bugger, Joe." I said, "What are you talking about?" He said, "Do you remember that first night outside the Rotunda? Lee Wilson?" "I do remember," I said, "I'll never forget it." "Well we got him today in Gorey."'

The next morning, Elizabeth O'Farrell – by then nicknamed the 'Sinn Féin nurse' by the soldiers – recommenced handing out the surrender orders. Accompanied by three soldiers in a car, including an unarmed Capt. de Courcy-Wheeler, she carried an old white apron on a stick as a flag of truce.

She went first to St Stephen's Green, where shooting was so frequent that cross-fire at Grafton Street meant that she had to leave the car and approach the College of Surgeons on foot. Having delivered the surrender order, she then returned to the car, which made its way towards Boland's mill. As there was still sniping in the area, her army driver refused to take her through the firing line and O'Farrell had to continue on foot. 'I started through the firing line from Butt Bridge to Boland's. I did not know whether the Volunteers were still in Boland's or not, so I had to go up Westland Row to the military to ask them to locate the Volunteers for me. This was a very difficult job and I had to take my life in my hands several times.' At one spot on the road, she saw two loaves of bread and a hat caked in blood. Crossing Grand Canal Street Bridge a man walking just behind her was shot.

And her arrest moments after leaving the College of Surgeons. This photograph was kept in de Courcy-Wheeler's papers.

She finally located Éamon de Valera in a dispensary that he was using as a headquarters. It was a week during which nervous exhaustion had taken its toll as an expected assault by the military never arrived. On the Friday, de Valera had even ordered the men to leave Boland's for the nearby railway embankment, from where they watched the city burning before de Valera decided to reoccupy Boland's.

When O'Farrell arrived, de Valera at first thought that it was a hoax, but finally agreed to surrender if he first received orders from Thomas MacDonagh.

MacDonagh was in Jacob's, another place that had little influence on the battle. O'Farrell returned to the army car and travelled there next. While she went to make contact with the

British troops pose with a captured rebel flag. 132 members of the government forces were killed in the fighting.

The GPO as it was after the surrender of the rebels. Having begun the week filled with bank holiday crowds going about their ordinary business in fine weather, the building had ended it as an enduring symbol of the 1916 Rising.

IRISH DISQUIET ON THE WESTERN FRONT

On the Western Front in the First World War, there were plenty of Irish fighting with the British forces during Easter week 1916 who would have considered themselves to be nationalists. Indeed many were National Volunteers fighting for the promise of Home Rule, and who enlisted as a response to John Redmond's rallying call.

Tom Kettle, a Nationalist MP and poet, had even travelled on an arms-raising mission to Germany in 1913, before joining the 16th (Irish) Division. Willie Redmond (brother of John) was another Nationalist MP who died during the war. The poet Francis Ledwidge was a close friend of Thomas MacDonagh, but died while serving in the Inniskilling Fusiliers.

However many of the Irish empathised with the cause of Irish independence, there seems to have been very little support among the troops for the rebellion. Many, in fact, felt betrayed. Capt. Stephen Gwynn, a Nationalist MP serving in France, said that his men 'felt they had been stabbed in the back'.

The Germans attempted to demoralise the Irish soldiers serving on the Western Front by passing out placards. One announced the fall of Kut to the Turkish, while the other

Eiríge Amać Seaċtṁaine na Cásga, 1916

EASTER WEEK RISING, 1916

Boland's Mills Garrison

SIGNATURES

The signatures of the men of Éamon de Valera's Boland's mill garrison. They had seen comparatively little action. On the Friday, de Valera had even ordered the men to leave Boland's for the nearby railway embankment, from where they watched the city burning before de Valera decided to reoccupy Boland's.

SUNDAY
23

MONDAY
24

TUESDAY
25

WEDNESDAY
26

THURSDAY
27

FRIDAY
28

SATURDAY
29

rebel leader, Capt. de Courcy-Wheeler drove to the front door of the College of Surgeons to take the surrender there. Among those inside was Constance Markievicz, who was a cousin of Wheeler's wife.

'A white flag was hanging out of the door of the college. Two of the rebel leaders came out, advanced, and saluted. The commandant stated that he was Michael Mallin and that his companion was Countess Markievicz. That he and the garrison wished to surrender.

'The Countess was dressed in the uniform of an Irish Volunteer, green breeches, putties, tunic, and slouch hat with feathers and Sam Browne belt, with arms and ammunition. I asked her would she wish to be driven in my motor car under escort to the Castle, knowing the excitement her appearance would create when marching through the streets. She said: "No, I shall march at the head of my men as I am second in command, and shall share their fate."

'Accordingly, I requested her to disarm, which she did. When handing over her arms she kissed her small revolver reverently.'

Around this time, James Stephens was looking in the direction of Jacob's. 'It is half-past three o'clock, and from my window the Republican flag can still be seen flying over Jacob's factory. There is occasional shooting, but the city as a whole is quiet. At a quarter to five o'clock a heavy gun boomed once. Ten minutes later there was heavy machine gun firing and much rifle shooting. In another 10 minutes the flag at Jacob's was hauled down.'

Thomas MacDonagh, having demanded and received a meeting with General Lowe, had then gone to inform Eamonn Ceannt at the South Dublin Union.

At the nearby Marrowbone Lane, Robert Holland and the other rebels had actually started the day in a good mood. They had heard that 'the troops which had come from England had suffered very heavy losses and were completely beaten and were in complete confusion all around Dublin.

read 'Irishmen! Heavy uproar in Ireland. English guns are firing at your wives and children.' A raiding party crawled through no man's land to capture the placards, and it was reported that Irish soldiers responded to the German taunts by singing Irish songs and 'Rule Britannia'. While some British officers made mention of the Irish soldiers' continuing commitment to the fight after the Easter Rising, the event did exacerbate the suspicion already felt towards the nationalist Irish serving in the British Army. Tom Kettle had prophesised that the Easter rebels 'will go down to history as heroes and martyrs, and I will go down – if I go down at all – as a bloody British officer'.

Many of the veterans returned home to Ireland to find a changed political landscape. In all, between 25,000 and 35,000 Irish-born soldiers died in the First World War. However, many of the soldiers who returned to an increasingly nationalist Ireland received a cold and sometimes hostile welcome. Kettle's words were soon borne out as the veterans and the dead of the First World War were not only overshadowed by the people and events of the Easter Rising, but would soon find that their contribution to the British cause was considered somewhat shameful in a newly independent Ireland.

Éamon de Valera after his surrender. When Nurse O'Farrell arrived, de Valera first thought that it was a hoax, but finally agreed to surrender if he first received orders from Thomas MacDonagh.

'We were still in the best of spirits and the girls had baked some cakes and were getting ready for the céilídhe in the Main Hall which had previously been cleared. We were looking forward to this when at about 6pm a despatch came from Commandant Eamonn Ceannt at the South Dublin Union which was the headquarters of the 4th Battalion. We were told that this despatch had come from Ceannt and it was to the effect that no one was to fire on any British soldier he would see in uniform without first reporting to one of the officers. A rumour went around that a truce was being called.'

Éamon de Valera, marked with an 'x', leads his men away from Boland's mill after the surrender. He would be the only leader of the Rising not to be executed.

At 6.30pm Ceannt, with a clergyman and a British officer, entered the front gate of the Marrowbone distillery and spoke with the rebel leaders there. When finished, Holland asked Con Colbert for an explanation. 'He said it was all over. When I heard this I felt kind of sick in my stomach, putting it mildly, and everybody else felt the same, I'm sure. It came as a great shock. Colbert could hardly speak as he stood in the yard for a moment or two. He was completely stunned. The tears rolled down his cheeks.' Colbert blew a whistle and ordered the men of the distillery to 'fall in' to double file. While this was happening, one of the men in the rear dropped his shotgun, which went off and wounded another rebel.

Colbert told them they were surrendering unconditionally, but that anyone wishing to escape could do so. Holland remembers one rebel, Joe McGrath (later of Hospitals Trust and its famous sweepstakes), saying 'Toor-a-loo, boys, I'm off', and then leaving. Some others followed.

'Then Colbert reformed us up, numbered us off and we "sloped arms" and we marched out of the Distillery through the front entrance with Colbert at our head. A lot of men had gathered around outside and I heard Eamonn Ceannt distinctly say, "Where were you men when you were wanted?"'

The rebels, numbering over a hundred men, were marched in military formation from Marrowbone Lane, into Cork Street, the Coombe, Patrick Street and Bride Street, towards their destination of Richmond Barracks in Inchicore. 'On our route we were subjected to very ugly remarks and cat-calls from the poorer classes,' remembered Holland, who also watched a farcical occurrence during the march. 'When we were almost at the Coombe Maternity Hospital, two drunken men insisted in falling in with us. They were ejected from our ranks several times on the route but eventually must have got into the ranks in my rear, for about two months later I saw those two men taking their exercise in Knutsford Prison.'

As the rebels arrived onto Bride Road, British soldiers with fixed bayonets formed up two deep on each path. 'They had machine guns posted at Bride Street and facing us and the military then closed in behind us. Orders were given for us to halt and people were ordered to get away from the windows of the buildings on each side and to close them.'

Put into double file, they were ordered to lay down their arms on the road. 'A military lorry was then passed down behind us and soldiers started to throw our rifles and revolvers into the lorry. A few shots went off as a few of the late owners had forgotten to extract the cartridges.'

The rebels themselves formed the smallest category of those who had died in the fighting since Monday. Of them, 62 had died, compared to 132 members of government forces. A large majority of the dead – 256 people – were uninvolved civilians who had been caught in crossfire or shelling or deliberately shot by combatants on either side. On their march, then, the surrendered rebels were subjected to continual abuse from the public.

'They were "Shoot the Sinn Féin ****s." My name was called out by some boys and girls I had gone to school with … The British troops saved us from manhandling. This was the first time I ever appreciated the British troops as they undoubtedly saved us from being manhandled that evening and I was very glad as I walked in the gate of Richmond Barracks.'

Inside Richmond Barracks, Holland and his colleagues 'were packed choked full into a billet and three or four buckets were left in to act as latrines. The door was locked and we had hardly any room to sit down. We were in this room all night. Everyone seemed to be in serious thought and no one wanted to converse as we were practically jammed tight together. Someone suggested that as one side of the room tightened the other half might get room to sit down and rest for a while. This was done.'

Holland wondered aloud as to what would become of them now. Some thought that they might be shipped to the Western Front; others that they would be sent to the colonies, or executed.

'After a pause Colbert spoke. He said that from his point of view he would prefer to be executed and said "we are all ready to meet our God. We had hopes of coming out alive. Now that we are defeated, outside that barrack wall the people whom we have tried to emancipate have demonstrated nothing but hate and contempt for us. We would be better off dead as life would be a torture. We can thank the Mother of God for her kindness in her intercession for us that we have had the time to prepare ourselves to meet our Redeemer."

'Colbert then called us all to recite the Rosary for the spiritual and temporal welfare of those who fought and died in the cause of Irish Freedom, past, present and future generations. We were in darkness and remembering no more, I fell asleep.'

AFTERMATH

- Arrests begin, and many without rebel connections are held.

- Details of outrages are made public, including the murder of Francis Sheehy Skeffington.

- Courts martial commence on May 2nd.

- Pearse, MacDonagh and Clarke are executed the following day.

- By May 12th, 15 are executed.

- Public revulsion at the harsh treatment of leaders combines with antagonism to conscription.

On the night of May 7th, just hours before his execution, Michael Mallin, who had commanded the Citizen Army at St Stephen's Green, wrote to his wife of how he had passed their house, a few hundred yards from Kilmainham Gaol, as he was being led from Richmond Barracks to his final destination. He hoped to catch sight of his 'darling Wife, Pulse of my heart' or their four young children.

'The only one of my household that I could cast my longing Eyes on was poor Prinnie the dog she looked so faithfull (sic) there at the door ... I am so cold this has been a such a cruel week.'

Mallin tried to keep up a brave front, but the reality of impending death, and of his departure from his wife and children shattered him: 'My heartstrings are torn to pieces when I think of you and them of our manly James happy go lucky John shy warm Una dadys (sic) Girl and oh little Joseph my little man my little man Wife dear Wife I cannot keep the tears back when I think of him he will rest in my arms no more ... my little man my little man my little man, his name unnerves me again all your dear faces arise before me God bless you God bless you my darlings ...'

Prisoners held at Wellington Barracks during Easter Week. Major John MacBride is sixth from the right. William Cosgrave remembered how MacBride had told him that 'his life-long prayer had been answered. He said three Hail Marys every day that he should not die until he had fought the British in Ireland.'

In the context of a vicious war, it was probably inevitable that the British authorities would mete out the ultimate punishment to at least some of those who had attacked their forces and openly declared an alliance with the enemy. In the context of Irish history, it was perhaps equally inevitable that those reprisals would alienate much of Irish opinion. Most Irish and even many British politicians understood this, but with martial law in force and Sir John Maxwell installed as military governor, political subtleties were never likely to dominate the official response.

In the immediate aftermath of the Rising, the authorities arrested 3,430 men and 79 women thought to be 'Sinn Féiners'. (A term used by the authorities to describe the militant Volunteers, even though few were members of Sinn Féin.) The accuracy of the intelligence on which the arrests were based can be judged from the fact that 1,424 were released within a fortnight, and all but 579 were subsequently released on the grounds that they posed no

British cavalry on the Dublin quays in the aftermath of the Rising.

danger to the state. Even some of those who were deported, along with the veterans of the Rising, to English prisons and the Frongoch detention camp in Wales had no previous involvement in violent nationalism. The main effect of the arrests, therefore, was to alienate nationalist opinion. At the same time, details began to emerge of British atrocities, including the murders of Francis Sheehy Skeffington and other innocent civilians. The revelations undermined the assumption of moral superiority that, for the authorities, justified the executions of the leaders of the Rising.

Of the rebel prisoners, 186 men and one woman (Constance Markievicz) were selected to be tried by military court martial, to be held at Richmond Barracks. (Because of his injuries, James Connolly was tried in the military hospital at Dublin Castle.) The first courts martial sat on May 2nd and immediately sentenced three men – Patrick Pearse, Tom Clarke and Thomas MacDonagh – to death. The three were taken that evening to the disused

THE BEGINNING OF THE END

The Proclamation of an Irish Republic from the steps of the GPO did not exactly ring around the world in April 1916, but it did start a long drawn-out process of dismantlement of the then mighty British Empire. The 1916 Rebellion had, after all, been ruthlessly suppressed by British power just as stirrings of revolt in the colonies from time to time were stamped out.

But the Anglo-Irish Treaty of 1921 showed independence movements, especially in India, that it was possible to win a measure of freedom from the imperial power. If Ireland, which was an integral part of the United Kingdom, could progress to the status of a self-governing dominion, surely the faraway colonies could aspire to this kind of freedom also.

By achieving dominion status instead of the sought-after republic, the Irish Free State joined Canada, Australia, New Zealand and South Africa as partners in the British Commonwealth. Allegiance was due to the king, who was represented by a governor-general in the dominions, but in practice these countries were independent, although Britain preferred to be vague about what this meant constitutionally.

The Free State pushed Britain hard to spell out the independent status of the dominions at imperial conferences in the 1920s and 1930s, at which Ireland was represented by ministers such as Kevin O'Higgins and Patrick McGilligan. In 1926, the Balfour Declaration defined dominions as 'autonomous Communities within the British Empire, equal in status, in no way subordinate one to another in any aspect of their domestic or external affairs though united by a common allegiance to the Crown, and freely associated as members of the British Commonwealth of Nations'.

The Statute of Westminster in 1931 spelled out the implications further. McGilligan declared that the imperial system, which it had taken centuries to build, had been demolished. He was referring, of course, only to the white dominions and not to the British colonies all around the world. In Asia these included India, Burma, Malaysia, Hong Kong, Borneo; in Africa there was Uganda, Kenya, Anglo-Egyptian Sudan, Somalia, Northern and Southern Rhodesia, Bechuanaland, Nigeria, Cameroons, Gold Coast, Togo, Sierra Leone and Gambia; in the Caribbean there were numerous islands including Jamaica, Bahamas, Barbados, Trinidad and Grenada.

The Free State ministers had played a leading role in securing an independent status for the dominions but it was Éamon de Valera coming to power in 1932 who exploited this freedom. He proceeded to abolish the Oath of Allegiance and the office of governor-general, to take the king out of the 1922 Constitution and to remove international relations from any British tutelage. He deliberately left the crown with a technical role in the accrediting of diplomats.

The 1937 Constitution completed the process and made Ireland into a republic in all but name. This attracted the close attention of the Congress party in India, some of whose leaders visited Dublin to meet de Valera. The Irish example showed India could be a republic and also in the Commonwealth. The value of Ireland's increasing emancipation from Britain was clearly shown when the Second World War broke out. Ireland declared its neutrality while the British viceroy, Lord Linlithgow, declared war on behalf of India without consulting any Indian political leaders.

India and Pakistan became independent in 1948 as republics within the Commonwealth. Ironically, Ireland a year later formally declared itself a republic and left the Commonwealth. This was not done by de Valera but by the all-party government which came to power in 1948 hoping 'to take the gun out of Irish politics'.

The Second World War and its aftermath speeded up the disintegration of the British, French and Dutch empires. In a speech in Cape Town in 1960, the British prime minister, Harold Macmillan, warned that the 'winds of change' were blowing for the African continent. Ghana (formerly Gold Coast and Togo) had become independent in 1957. The decolonisation of the rest of the British Empire in Africa followed soon afterwards.

The map of the world with the large swathes coloured in the red of the British Empire on which 'the sun never sets' was history by 1966, just 50 years after the Easter Rising. Those first shots in Dublin were the start of the process, but how much they influenced it can still be debated.

Kilmainham Gaol and shot at dawn on May 3rd in the Stonebreaker's Yard. Clarke, who had spent a quarter of his 58 years in prison for IRB activities, told his wife during the night that he was 'relieved' that he was going to be executed because his greatest dread was that he would be sent back to prison again.

Immediately after the executions of Pearse, Clarke and MacDonagh, the Irish Party leader, John Redmond, warned the prime minister, Herbert Asquith, that 'if any more executions take place in Ireland, the position will become impossible for any Constitutional Party or leader'. Asquith himself warned Sir John Maxwell that 'anything like a large number of executions would … sow the seeds of lasting trouble in Ireland'. But Maxwell kept the executions going, even after May 8th when the prominent Irish Party politician, John Dillon, told him that 'it really would be difficult to exaggerate the amount of mischief the executions are doing'.

That mischief was stressed, too, by the most famous Irishman in Britain, the playwright and controversialist Bernard Shaw. In a prescient letter to the *London Daily News*, published on May 10th, he wrote that up to 'the very eve of the present rising I used all my influence and power to discredit the Sinn Féin ideal' but maintained nevertheless that 'an Irishman resorting to arms to achieve the independence of his country is doing only what Englishmen will do if it is their misfortune to be invaded and conquered by the Germans in the course

How the press covered the executions, with the Sunday Pictorial *particularly keen on the story that Joseph Plunkett had married Grace Gifford in Kilmainham Gaol before his execution on May 4th.*

of the present war'. Thus, he argued, the executions would turn the rebels into heroes: 'It is absolutely impossible to slaughter a man in this position without making him a martyr and a hero, even though the day before the rising he may only have been a minor poet. The shot Irishmen will now take their places beside Emmet and the Manchester Martyrs in Ireland, and beside the heroes of Poland and Serbia and Belgium in Europe; and nothing in heaven or earth can prevent it ... The military authorities and the British Government must have known that they were canonising their prisoners. But they said in their anger: "We don't care; we will shoot them; we feel that way." Similarly the Irish will reply: "We knew you would; you always do; we simply tell you more or less politely *how we* feel about it."'

(A week earlier, Shaw had written an acerbic private letter to under-secretary Nathan, sarcastically decrying the failure of the British artillery assault to at least demolish the notorious Dublin slums: 'Why didn't the artillery knock down half Dublin whilst it had the chance? Think of the insanitary areas, the slums, the glorious chance of making a clean sweep of them! Only 179 houses, and probably at least nine of them quote decent ones. I'd have laid at least 17,900 of them flat and made a decent town of it.')

The courts martial were held in secret, at least partly because, after a chaotic week, it was extremely difficult for the authorities to present detailed evidence against specific individuals. According to one of those tried, William Cosgrave, 'my recollection is that we were assembled into groups and ushered into the Court, consisting of three senior officers. The President of the Court, or the Crown Prosecutor, Lieutenant Wylie, informed us we

Grace Gifford, who married Joseph Plunkett in the hours before his execution. A member of Cumann na mBan, she would herself spend time in Kilmainhaim Gaol later in 1916.

were being tried by Field-General Courtmartial. No person was allowed to appear and speak on behalf of the prisoner, but each prisoner would be permitted to bring a friend with him, who he could consult and who would be free to advise the prisoner but not address the Court.'

The charges were laid according to a formula: 'You are charged with having been one of a party at [whatever location] from which shots were fired, occasioning casualties amongst His Majesty's troops, and you are further charged with conspiracy with His Majesty's enemies.' The evidence against many of the rebels was deeply confused, however. Those who fought at the South Dublin Union and Marrowbone Lane were charged with having been in

Because of his injuries, James Connolly was tried in the military hospital at Dublin Castle and was executed while seated in a chair.

Jacob's factory. According to Cosgrave, 'Captain Rotheram, one of the best known and most popular sportsmen of the County Westmeath, the best polo-player at No. 1 in Ireland, took the surrender of the Volunteers at South Dublin Union and Marrowbone Lane, and marched with the prisoners to Bride Road. He was called upon the following day to give evidence of the surrender in both places. His reply was that he had not seen these men yesterday, that he did not know them, not having seen them before, that he would not know them again; that he would not feel justified in giving testimony. It is but fair to say that his sight had become impaired, which was the reason assigned for his relinquishing polo.'

HOW *THE IRISH TIMES* COVERED THIS 'DESPERATE EPISODE'

For the early days of the Easter Rising, *The Irish Times* had the field all to itself thanks to having its office south of the Liffey. The rival *Irish Independent* and the *Freeman's Journal* were in the thick of the action beside the GPO and could not publish. The *Freeman's Journal* premises on Prince's Street was burned down. The *Daily Express* office in Cork Street opposite City Hall was actually occupied on Easter Monday by the rebels, and 26 of them eventually died there.

The Irish Times office was at 31 Westmoreland Street, near Trinity College and the Bank of Ireland. The paper had an independent power supply from its suction gas plant. The coverage of the fighting in Dublin was a tribute to the reporters who had to work under very dangerous conditions. The trade paper, *Newspaper World*, later paid tribute to *The Irish Times* for its coverage 'of the memorable week when the continuing rifle and Maxim gunfire in the Westmoreland Street area made it impossible to venture around. Members of the several departments in the office were in attendance on each day but the paper was not published on the Friday and Saturday.' The paper made up for this temporary gap with a Special Extra edition on May 1st.

On the Tuesday after the Rising, the paper reported on how the insurgents had occupied strategic buildings around the city, the resistance they met, the number of casualties and the beginning of the looting in O'Connell Street by what was termed the 'Dublin underworld'.

A 'most shocking' event for the paper was the attack on the unarmed 'Veterans' Corps' coming back from a route march in the Dublin Mountains to Beggar's Bush Barracks, where they were shot down by the insurgents stationed on the railway bridge and in houses around. The reporters and sub-editors were unsure how to describe the insurgents who were referred to variously as 'volunteers', 'rebels', 'Sinn Féiners' and 'revolutionists'.

Editorially, the newspaper had no doubt where it stood. On the Tuesday, the editorial, entitled 'The Outbreak', thundered that 'an attempt has been made to overthrow the constitutional Government of Ireland'. This 'desperate episode in Irish history can have only one end', and the editor was trusting firmly on a 'speedy triumph of the forces of law and order'.

At this early stage, before Sackville Street (later O'Connell Street) had been partially demolished, the paper tried to show that normal life in Dublin was carrying on. The main news item was the opening of the Spring Show at the Royal Dublin Society in Ballsbridge and readers were also told about the latest production of the D'Oyly Carte company and the opening of the Feis Ceoil.

More space was devoted in the first days to the conduct of the First World War in Europe, the Middle East and Africa than to the Rising. The Irish casualties in these battles were highlighted.

The restrictions on non-combatants in Dublin following the imposition of martial law prompted an *Irish Times* reporter to suggest to readers how to cope with having to stay at home instead of promenading around the streets in the evening. The father could 'cultivate a habit of easy conversation with his family' or 'put his little garden into a state of decency', do some 'useful painting and mending about the house' or 'acquire or re-acquire the art of reading', and who better then Shakespeare given that it was the tercentenary of his death?

As the fighting and destruction intensified, the reporters tried to stay detached and factual but there was no denying where their sympathies lay. Thus 'Trinity College, Dublin, in the crisis, proved true to its traditions ... the spirit of the few collegians who happened to be within the gates was indomitable ... every graduate who could be rounded up answered the call.' It was 'surely a sign that Trinity had given itself wholly over to the military when one found soldiers playing football on the tennis courts.'

Some Trinity students helped prepare the artillery for the shelling of Liberty Hall which the newspaper described as being 'for many years a thorn in the side of the Dublin police and the Irish government. It was the centre of social anarchy in Ireland, the brain of every riot and disturbance'. The students also captured a 'Larkinite' spy who had infiltrated the campus.

There was also praise for the behaviour of the volunteers in the area of the Adelaide Hospital, where some of their wounded had been brought for treatment. 'The insurgents in that part of the city seemed to be of a good type. No sign of liquor was ever observed on them and they were invariably courteous, while they refrained from abusing the convalescent soldiers in the hospital.'

By the time of the Special Extra edition on the Monday after the Rising, the insurgents had surrendered the previous Saturday, so the editorial, entitled 'The Insurrection', got down to analysing what it called 'a record of crime, horror and destruction' by one side but 'shot with many gleams of the highest valour and devotion' on the side of the 'gallant soldiers'. The editorial did 'not deny a certain desperate courage to many of the wretched men who today are in their graves or awaiting the sentence of their country's laws.'

For this last category, 'The State has struck but its work is not yet finished. The surgeon's knife has been put to the corruption in the body of Ireland and its course must not be stayed until the whole malignant growth has been removed.' Was this a call for the execution of those the paper called the 'ring-leaders' and the 'arch-conspirators'?

The rival *Freeman's Journal*, when it re-appeared on May 5th, saw it as a 'bloodthirsty incitement' to the government. *The Irish Times* rejected this charge but later in the week made clear it supported the British prime minister, Herbert Asquith, when he refused to call for a stop to the executions while the last two signatories of the Proclamation still alive, James Connolly and Seán MacDermott, were awaiting their fate.

Across the river, the *Irish Independent* was back on the streets after a 10-day break, and in its editorial of May 10th pleaded for leniency for those who filled 'only minor parts'.

'When, however, we come to some of the ringleaders, instigators and fomentors not yet dealt with, we must make an exception.' It was clear to readers that Connolly, who had been a bugbear to the proprietor of the *Independent* and of the Dublin tramway company, William Martin Murphy, was being referred to. 'Let the worst of the ringleaders be singled out and dealt with as they deserve.' Whether this reflected the views of the mainly Catholic business class and clerical readers of the paper is hard to know. Connolly and MacDermott were shot two days later.

The editor of *The Irish Times* must have been gratified by the letter in the edition of May 12th in which a reader wished 'to express my recognition of, and gratitude for, the fearless way in which you are daily giving correct expression to the views of all loyal Irish people in this deplorable crisis'.

The demand for *The Irish Times* was so great that it reprinted the issues of Easter Week when it was the only newspaper to be had. The *Weekly Irish Times* came out with a triple issue dated April 29th, May 6th and 13th. This issue contained a complete record of the Rising with full details of the fighting, lists of casualties and prisoners, sentences and deportations and pictures of the main personalities. The paper boasted that the issue was 'enormously popular and had a colossal circulation which far exceeded anything ever previously claimed by any Dublin newspaper, morning, evening or weekly'. (The *Weekly Irish Times* was a companion to the daily title, taking a longer look at the events of the week gone by. Often bought to send to family members abroad, it continued to be published until 1941, when it was replaced by the *Times Pictorial*.)

A year later, in 1917, The *Weekly Irish Times* published the 286-page Sinn Féin Rebellion Handbook, which reproduced the contemporary reports of the Rising and its aftermath with maps. But it also included later accounts of the courts martial, Roger Casement's landing, capture, trial and execution, two commissions of enquiry, full lists of those killed, taken prisoner, honours and promotions. It is an amazingly comprehensive account of every aspect of the Rising. It was republished in 1988 in facsimile form and is now a collector's item.

A British soldier points at the spot in the Stonebreaker's Yard of Kilmainham Gaol where Patrick Pearse and his fellow leaders were executed. Predicting his death, Pearse had written to his mother on May 1st, saying 'we do not expect that they will spare the lives of the leaders'.

A depiction of one of the executions. Blindfolds were offered, and a regulation white square was placed above the condemned man's heart as a target for the firing squad.

Many of the prisoners had little idea what to expect. Some of the leaders, including Patrick Pearse and Thomas MacDonagh, knew even before their trials that they would be killed. Pearse wrote to his mother on May 1st that he hoped his followers would be spared, but 'we do not expect that they will spare the lives of the leaders'. Con Colbert, feeling depressed in Richmond Barracks, actually expressed the hope that he would be shot. He told Robert Holland that 'from his point of view he would prefer to be executed and said, "We are all ready to meet our God. We had hopes of coming out alive. Now that we are defeated, outside that barrack wall the people whom we tried to emancipate have demonstrated nothing but hate and contempt for us. We would be better off dead as life would be a torture."'

Relatives and friends hand supplies to the rebels housed in Richmond Barracks. Allowed to visit three times a week, they would bring food and letters.

British Prime Minister Herbert Asquith (centre) arrives at Kingstown (now Dún Laoghaire) on May 12th. By the time of his visit, the executions had seen public opinion swing in favour of the rebels – a situation Asquith had predicted.

Maurice Collins spoke to Seán MacDermott in Richmond Barracks: 'On the morning we had received orders from the British that we were to be deported I was standing beside Seán MacDermott in the Barracks Square and said to him "It looks, Seán, as if we will be all together wherever we are going this time." He replied "No Maurice, the next place you and I will meet will be in heaven." Up to that he had not been courtmartialled and I could not understand why he passed this remark.'

INTERNMENT

In the immediate period after the Rising 3,430 men and 79 women suspected of being 'Sinn Féiners' were taken into custody. However, as it became clear that not all of those who sympathised with the Irish nationalism actually took an active part in the rebellion many were released. Within a fortnight, 1,424 of the men and been sent home. Of those remaining, 159 men and one woman, Constance Markievicz, were court-martialled. But many more were interned without ever being sentenced.

On the Monday morning – a week after the Rising had begun – Robert Holland was among those waking up in a packed room in Richmond Barracks.

'It was daylight when my brother, Dan, woke me up. I was cramped and stiff. The barrack-room door was open and the soldiers of the guard were handing in some half-pound tins of bully beef. They were being passed over the heads of those in front to the lads at the back with the order that two men were to divide each tin and to keep the tin as it would act as a mug to drink the tea with. We then got four dog biscuits each, Dan and myself staying together. After the meal an armed escort of about eight soldiers came to the door and an NCO called out "Twenty men for the latrines".'

Once all this was completed, the rebels were paraded about the square, their names and occupations were taken and they were then sent to gymnasium hall. All those under the age of 18 were offered the chance to go home, although not all took that opportunity.

Police detectives picked out suspected leaders, including Eamonn Ceannt, Con Colbert, Major John MacBride and William T. Cosgrave. After two hours, as Holland put it, 'Those of us who were left must have looked a very squalid sight as now our leaders and intellectuals had been taken away from us.'

On Tuesday evening, all of those in Robert Holland's room were brought from Richmond Barracks and marched to the North Wall. 'We were put into the hold of a cattleboat as that was the kind of smell that was in it. As the last of us got in, the lights were switched off and we found ourselves locked in. We had got no rations leaving Richmond Barracks and the only thing we next knew was the boat moving and we were out to sea being tossed about. A lot of others and myself got sick with the heat and foul smell and a torpedo or mine would have been a happy release.'

Holland was transported to Knutsford prison, one of several that was to house insurgents in the aftermath of the Easter Rising.

The rebels, as it turned out, had not been alone in the idea that they could be made repay the Empire by service on the Front. General Maxwell briefly touted the idea, only for the War Office to dismiss it. Instead, over 1,800 were sent to England and for a two-month period, the internees and prisoners were split between jails in Knutsford, Wakefield, Glasgow, Stafford, Reading and Wandsworth.

Oscar Traynor was also among those in Knutsford, and recalled afterwards that 'we were treated in a rather brutal fashion. My own personal experience for almost a month was that I was left without a bed or bedclothes. Near the end of the first month there was a complete change of attitude, and we were allowed to mix together, where before we were not allowed to approach nearer than five paces.'

That silence had been rigorously enforced, sometimes with periods of solitary confinement in darkness, leading to the prisoners having to use communicate in the Morse code they had learned during their training.

Frongoch camp in north Wales then became the main internment camp to which the men were transferred. Until then it had housed German prisoners of war in an abandoned distillery and crude huts, but these were moved to make way for the Irish prisoners. Here, the men could use the sports ground, hold concerts and several even became friendly with the guards. The men were woken by a hooter each morning at 5.30am, dinner was at 12.30pm and lights out was at 8.20pm. Initially they stayed in 35 huts, each of which held a maximum of 30 men. Two lanes running through the centre of the huts were named Pearse Street and Connolly Street.

However, in putting these men together in one place, the British were inadvertently helping to organise the nationalists in a structured environment that would not have been otherwise possible. The gathering of so many rebels in one spot meant that many men learned the guerrilla tactics that would be used in the later War of Independence, because of which Frongoch gained the nickname 'University of Revolution'. The few months of its existence would prove crucial in the years to come.

An internee, Thomas Leahy, recalled how, 'classes were formed on every subject in everyday life that would be expected of us under the law under the Republic. We hoped to confirm at the first chance after release all departments of government business, and instructions to fit men capable to take over these departments when required.'

It was quickly seen as an opportunity as much as an imposition. 'Had the British government known what was taking place under their own guard and officials, we would have been hunted out of the camp, for it must be realised that men came together in that camp from all parts of Ireland; from towns, villages and places that would have taken years to bring together for the work which had to be done, especially in the training of the army of the Republic.'

An Advisory Committee was set up by the government with the aim of interviewing each internee to determine whether they deserved to be imprisoned or not. Rather than interview the men in Wales, an arduous process saw up to 60 internees at a time brought instead to Wandsworth and Wormwood Scrubs prisons.

Suspicious of the information being sought of them during interviews that might last only a few minutes, the men occasionally confused their interrogators. One man demanded that he be allowed answer only in Irish, but when a translator was brought in it turned out that he could speak only Scots Gaelic. When an Irish speaker was found, the internee confused matters further by speaking only in an Aran Islands dialect.

All but 573 were released by this committee, with the freed men returned to Ireland on early morning ferries in order to minimise the welcome they might receive.

Attempts were made to weed out the large proportion of men who, because they were born in England or Scotland, qualified for conscription. However, prisoners refused to co-operate and whole-scale punishment followed.

Gradually, the conditions in the camp began to become a focus of protest. Hunger strikes became a weapon of dissent. The internees refused to work in a local quarry, and also refused a request by the camp's commander, Colonel F.A. Heygate Lambert, to not only empty their own latrines but also those of their guards.

When, as a punitive measure, the camp was split into North and South, the conditions in the latter – a disused distillery – were particularly poor. Irish MPs, the most vocal of which was Alfie Byrne, began to press for an improvement in the conditions. There were parliamentary questions, newspaper stories and a succession of inquiries which eventually became critical of Frongoch. Possibly because he was caught between his oath as a doctor and his responsibilities to the authorities (he had been ordered not to treat hunger strikers), the camp's medical officer was affected so much that he drowned himself.

Although they had left Dublin in disgrace, the prisoners who returned to the city from prison and internment camps at the end of 1916 and beginning of 1917 were given heroes' receptions, with many carried shoulder

It was the opportunity for organisation that new prime minister, Lloyd George, gave as his reason for the decision before Christmas 1916 to release the internees. He also agreed to release almost three dozen nationalist prisoners who had been held at Reading Jail in the belief that they were especially dangerous. Among these were future Irish president Seán T. O'Kelly and future president of Dáil Éireann, Arthur Griffith, and these prisoners had also held classes and planned for the future republic.

Men such as Éamon de Valera and Thomas Ashe, who had seen their death sentences commuted, were among those who remained in Lewes Prison. Here they also planned for revolution and engaged in hunger strikes. A prisoner Joe McGuinness won a parliamentary seat in a Longford by-election. Although this did not trigger his release, in June 1917 an unconditional amnesty was granted to the remaining Irish prisoners, including Constance Markievicz who was then locked up in Aylesbury Prison.

Put on a train from London, and a boat from Holyhead, the ex-convicts arrived at Dublin's Westland Row train station. Returning after a year's incarceration, the political climate in Ireland had altered substantially. The Irish question was up for discussion, the republican movement was gaining political momentum and the British government had shown itself open to conciliation. And these men who had left Dublin with the abuse of Dubliners stinging their ears were met on their return by a massive crowd, which swarmed around and lifted them shoulder high.

These expectations of death coloured the defiant stance taken by some of the leaders at their trials. Patrick Pearse made what the prosecutor William Wylie, a young barrister who was co-opted as deputy-advocate general, regarded as a 'Robert Emmet-type speech', and told his accusers that 'I went down on my knees as a child and told God that I would work all my life to gain the freedom of Ireland. I have divined it my duty as an Irishman to fight for the freedom of my Country.' James Connolly told his trial that 'I personally thank God that I have lived to see the day when thousands of Irish men and boys and hundreds of Irish women and girls' had been ready die in order to declare British rule in Ireland 'a crime against human progress'.

Some of the rank-and-file, on the other hand, feared that they would be sent off to the Western Front. One Volunteer, Martin Kavanagh, told Holland that '"I would not be surprised if we were shipped off to France" and elaborated on this. "We are all trained men; they must be in a bad way on the various fronts in France as the Germans were beating them on all sides and I am not surprised if the troops they have for replacement are of the same standard as those that have been sent against us ... They may divide us into small groups so that we will not be in a position to be of value to the Germans or detrimental to them."'

Asquith leaves Richmond Barracks after a visit. He had warned General Maxwell that 'anything like a large number of executions would ... sow the seeds of lasting trouble in Ireland'.

NORMALITY RETURNS SLOWLY

Services in Dublin took some time to recover after the Rising. On Friday, May 5th, *The Irish Times* reported that finally 'there were indications in almost every district of the city that Dublin is returning to normal condition. Shops and offices were opened in every street, and business seemed to be proceeding in the usual way. Except at a few points where "snipers" and suspected persons were supposed to be concealed in private houses there were very few soldiers on the streets.'

There had obviously been a few workers using the Rising as an excuse for a few days off of work. 'Movement about the city is now free – that is to say, no passes are required. On this account, no excuse remains for absence from employment, except, of course, in the cases of those whose places of employment have been destroyed or damaged beyond immediate repair. The authorities urge employees and workers in all occupations to return to work today, and they specify food, munitions and coal trades as those in which a full attendance of workers is particularly important. At the same time, people are requested not to loiter about the streets.'

NO REST FOR "THAT BRUTE MAXWELL"!

An illustration depicting General Maxwell being 'haunted' by his role in the executions. He had continued the executions despite the growing concern among the political establishment and revulsion among the general public.

Many of the rebels, however, seem to have expected relatively lenient treatment from the authorities. William Cosgrave reported 'some astonishment' among the prisoners at the sentencing of two men, Dick Davis and Seán McGarry, to eight years penal servitude. Even some of the most prominent leaders seem not to have expected a death sentence. According to Cosgrave, '[Eamonn] Ceannt had determined to make a fight for his life. [John] MacBride evidently thought he was facing a term of imprisonment, as he expressed to me his anxiety that his position as an official of the Dublin Corporation would be there for him on his release.'

These illusions were shared by some of the families of the rebel leaders and were prolonged by the often haphazard handling of the executions. The secrecy of the trials added to the confusion and the decision as to who would or would not be executed was at times arbitrary. Maxwell explained to Asquith that those to be executed would be either signatories of the Proclamation, commanding officers, or known murderers. But Willie Pearse, who was not among the leaders, seems to have been killed for no reason other than his relationship to his brother, Patrick. Eoin MacNeill was arrested and tried, even though he had tried to stop the Rising. Of the 90 death sentences handed down by the courts martial, moreover, all but 15 were commuted by Maxwell, among them that of Constance Markievicz, who, according to Wylie, had pleaded at her trial: 'I am only a woman, you cannot shoot a woman, you must not shoot

The mother of Patrick Pearse carries a wreath to her son's grave in June 1922. He was buried in quick lime in Arbour Hill. General Maxwell had refused to hand the leaders' bodies to their families for fear they would become shrines.

Willie Pearse, brother of Patrick, who was not among the leaders but was executed nonetheless, apparently because of his family connection.

a woman.' (Captain Harry de Courcy-Wheeler, who was staff captain to General Lowe and who gave evidence at Markievicz's trial, and who was distantly related to her by marriage, recorded, however, that she was defiant, and told the court martial 'I have no witnesses, what I did was for the freedom of Ireland and we thought we had a fighting chance.')

Some prisoners heard their comrades being shot and wondered if they themselves would be next. At daybreak on Friday morning, May 5th, William Cosgrave, whose cell in Kilmainham was next to that of Major John MacBride, 'heard a slight movement and whisperings in the Major's cell. After a few minutes there was a tap on his cell door. I heard the word "Sergeant", a few more whispers, a move towards the door of the cell, then steps down the corridor, down the central stairs. Through a chink in the door I could barely discern the receding figures; silence for a time; then the sharp crack of rifle fire; then silence again. I thought my turn would come next and waited for a rap on the door, but the firing squad had no further duty that morning.'

That afternoon, Cosgrave learned from a priest that his death sentence had been commuted. Shortly afterwards, however, 'two officers came to the door of the cell; enquired if my name was William Thomas Cosgrave, and on being told that it was so, one of them said "the decision of the Courtmartial is that you William Thomas Cosgrave have been found guilty and have been sentenced to death [by being] shot." Then a pause to see what the effect of the sentence would be. I remained silent. Then the officer continued, "the sentence has been commuted to penal servitude for life." I still think that they were surprised to find that my first reaction was an enquiry as to when I might be permitted to consult my solicitor.'

THE IRISH TIMES EDITORIAL
Tuesday, April 25th 1916
THE OUTBREAK

This newspaper has never been published in stranger circumstances than those which obtain to-day. An attempt has been made to overthrow the constitutional government of Ireland. It began yesterday morning in Dublin – at present we can speak for no other part of Ireland for there has been an abrupt stoppage of all means of external communication.

At this critical moment our language must be moderate, unsensational, and free from any tendency to alarm. As soon as peace and order have been restored the responsibility for this intended revolution will be fixed in the right quarter. The question whether it could have been averted will be discussed, and will be answered on the ample evidence which the events of the last few months afford. To-day we can deal only with today's and yesterday's facts. During the last twenty-four hours an effort has been made to set up an independent Irish Republic in Dublin. It was well organised; a large number of armed men are taking part in it; and to the general public, at any rate, the outbreak came as a complete surprise. An attempt was made to seize Dublin Castle but this failed. The rebels then took possession of the City Hall and of the Dublin *Daily Express* Office. During these operations a soldier and a policeman were shot dead. The General Post Office was seized and a green flag was hoisted on its roof. Several shops in this quarter of Sackville street were smashed and looted. It appears that the invaders of the Post Office have cut the telegraph and trunk telephone wires. Harcourt Street Station and Westland Row Station were seized; the South Dublin Union was seized. In the very centre of the city a party of the rebel volunteers took possession of St Stephen's Green, where, as we write, they are still entrenched. The military authorities were in motion soon after the beginning of the outbreak. Fierce fighting has taken place between the soldiers and the rebels in various parts of the city and there is reason to fear that many lives have been lost. The Fire Brigade ambulance was busy during yesterday and brought wounded soldiers and some wounded civilians to the various hospitals. The soldiers have retaken the City Hall and some other positions which were seized by the rebels; but, as we write, many places are still in rebel hands. Of course this desperate episode in Irish history can have only one end and the loyal public will await it as calmly and confidently as may be. Nothing in all yesterday's remarkable scenes was more remarkable than the quietness and courage with which the people of Dublin accepted the sudden and widespread danger. In the very neighbourhood of the fiercest fighting, the streets were full of cheerful or indifferent spectators. Such courage is excellent, but it may degenerate into recklessness.

Perhaps the most useful thing that we can do now is to remember that in quietness and confidence shall be our strength and to trust firmly in the speedy triumph of the forces of law and order. Those loyal citizens of Dublin who cannot actively help their country's cause at this moment may help it indirectly by refusing to give way to panic, and by maintaining in their households a healthy spirit of hope. The ordeal is severe but it will be short.

Prisoners Dick Donoghue and Tom Doyle being led to Kilmainham Gaol, escorted by British soldiers after the Rising. The British rounded up many more than had actually fought in the uprising.

For the families of prominent prisoners, the uncertainty created a roller-coaster of hope and fear. Michael O'Hanrahan's family was summoned to Kilmainham in the early hours of May 4th by a message from the authorities that he wished to see them 'before his deportation to England'. When they arrived at the jail, however, they met Kathleen Clarke and Ned Daly's sisters and were told that Daly was to be shot. 'We were horror-stricken, overcome, as we realised that the same fate must await our own brother.'

HELGA'S ROLES AFTER RISING

While the gunboat *Helga* is best-known as the ship that sailed up the Liffey and shelled Liberty Hall and the GPO, it had a role in another major incident two years later. It was one of the rescue ships that went to the assistance of RMS *Leinster*, the Dublin-Holyhead mail-boat, when it was torpedoed by a German U-boat on October 10th 1918.

On board the *Leinster* was a crew of 77 plus 680 passengers, 500 of whom were soldiers. When three torpedoes struck the ship 501 were killed, making it the greatest loss of life from a sinking in the Irish Sea.

The *Helga* was later bought by the Irish Free State and, having been renamed the LE *Muirchu*, became a fishery protection vessel until it was eventually scrapped in 1947.

Countess Markievicz, marked with an x, under arrest after the surrender. Originally sentenced to death for her role, along with 75 others this sentence was commuted.

THE IRISH TIMES EDITORIAL
April 28th and 29th and May 1st 1916
THE INSURRECTION

The 'Sinn Féin' Insurrection, which began on Easter Monday in Dublin, is virtually at an end. Desultory fighting continues in suburban districts. The severity of martial law is maintained; indeed, it is increased in the new Proclamation which we print to-day. Many streets and roads are still dangerous for the careless wayfarer. But the back of the insurrection is broken. Strong military forces skilfully directed by a strong hand, have decided the issue sooner than most of us had dared to hope. The cordon of troops which was flung round the city narrowed its relentless circle until further resistance became impossible. On Saturday, P.H. Pearse, one of the seven ring-leaders, surrendered unconditionally with the main body of the rebels. Yesterday other bodies came in dejectedly under the white flag. Of the buildings which were seized a week ago not one remains in rebel hands. The General Post Office, save for its noble portico, is a ruin. The premises of the Royal College of Surgeons and Messrs Jacob's factory were evacuated yesterday. St Stephen's Green was cleared on Thursday. Liberty Hall is no more than a sinister and hateful memory. It is believed that most of the ring-leaders are dead or captured. The outlaws who still 'snipe' from roofs may give a little more trouble, but their fate is certain. So ends the criminal adventure of the men who declared that they were 'striking in full confidence of victory,' and told their dupes that they would be 'supported by gallant allies in Europe.' The gallant ally's only gift to them was an Irish renegade whom it wanted to lose. Ireland has been saved from shame and ruin, and the whole Empire from a serious danger. Where our politicians failed – and worse than failed – the British Army has filled the breach and won the day. The Dublin Insurrection of 1916 will pass into history with the equally unsuccessful insurrections of the past. It will have only this distinction – that it was more daringly and systematically planned; and more recklessly invoked, than any of its predecessors.

The story of last week in Dublin is a record of crime, horror, and destruction, shot with many gleams of the highest valour and devotion. We do not deny a certain desperate courage to many of the wretched men who to-day are in their graves or awaiting the sentence of their country's laws. The real valour, however, and the real sacrifices were offered on the altar of Ireland's safety, and honour. The first tribute must be paid to the gallant soldiers who were poured into Dublin, including at least two battalions of famous Irish regiments. No courage could be finer than that of the young soldiers who, exhausted by a long voyage, and almost unrefreshed by sleep or food, were hurried straight into the hellish street-fighting of the last few days. Our veteran troops in France have seldom had to face a more fiery ordeal, and could hardly have done better than these lads fresh from the training camps. Again we testify to what we have seen when we praise the splendid devotion, not only of our Dublin doctors and nurses, but of the many civilians, men and women, who moved among the soldiers, bringing them food and drink in the hottest of the fray. The temper of the city as a whole has been admirable – cool and calm, without a moment's yielding to panic, but the cost of success has been terrible. Innocent civilians have been murdered in cold blood. The casualties among the troops have been heavy. The hospitals to-day report in all 152 dead, of whom 49 are soldiers. The destruction of property has been wanton and enormous. Between O'Connell Bridge and Nelson's Pillar a whole district of buildings, including the General Post Office, the Royal Hibernian Academy, and several of the most important business establishments in the city has vanished in flame. The loss is cruel and much of it is irreparable. Its chief burden will be felt, as such burdens are always chiefly felt, by the very poor. Many years must elapse before Dublin is herself again. This insurrection will leave behind it a long trail of sorrow, poverty and shame.

In the House of Commons last week Sir Edward Carson and Mr Redmond were at one in their desire that, so as long as the country remains in its present urgent danger, nobody should try to make political capital of the old, narrow kind out of these tragic events in Dublin. Until the danger is definitely at an end and we shall only say – and we are expressing the opinion of the whole world – that this outbreak, and all its deplorable consequences could have been averted. For the last year all Irishmen have known that the danger existed, and that it was coming surely and steadily to a head. Urgent and repeated warnings were given to the Government. They were neglected. The men who neglected them have accepted one of the gravest responsibilities in history. They will be called to account at the bar of public opinion and, when that time comes – and it must come soon – they will have to make their defence against a vast accumulation of damning evidence.

At the moment, however, it is more important to avoid possible mistakes than to call the inevitable to judgment. The crime has been committed; the explosion has occurred; and we have gained at least one advantage. We know now, beyond yea or nay, the extent, the power, the motives, and the methods of the seditious movement in Ireland. All the elements of disaffection have shown their hand. The State has struck, but its work is not yet finished. The surgeon's knife has been put to the corruption in the body of Ireland, and its course must not be stayed until the whole malignant growth has been removed. In the verdict of history weakness to-day would be even more criminal than the indifference of the last few months. Sedition must be rooted out of Ireland once for all. The rapine and bloodshed of the past week must be finished with a severity which will make any repetition of them impossible for generations to come. The loyal people of Ireland, Unionists and Nationalists call to-day with an imperious voice for the strength and firmness which have so long been strangers to the conduct of Irish affairs.

Arthur Griffith, considered the founder of Sinn Féin, played no part in the 1916 Rising but was arrested in its aftermath nonetheless.

Áine Ceannt believed, from a newspaper report on May 4th, that her husband Eamonn had been sentenced to just three years in prison. 'When I read this I was delighted.' Her sister-in-law told her, however, 'that I need not believe what I saw in the papers, that four more had been executed, Willie Pearse, Ned Daly, Michael O'Hanrahan and Joe Plunkett ... She also told me that the military escort sent for Mrs MacDonagh had failed to reach her, so that Mrs MacDonagh had no final interview with her husband.'

On Saturday, May 6th, Áine Ceannt managed to meet the Provost Marshal, Viscount Powerscourt, 'who was very amiable. He said he did not know what sentence these "gentlemen" got, but consented to give me a note to the Governor of Kilmainham, which permitted me to interview my husband. I arrived at Kilmainham, was shown in and found Eamonn in a cell with no seating accommodation and no bedding, not even a bed of straw. The first thing I noticed was that his Sam Browne belt was gone, and that his uniform was slightly torn. A sergeant stood at the door while we spoke, and could say very little, but I gathered from Eamonn that he had heard about the supposed three years' sentence and he felt it would worry me ... I said to him that the Rising was an awful fiasco, and he replied "No, it was the best thing since '98".'

The next day was 'a very wet day and I was sitting in the back room of my sister-in-law's house and my little son was in the front room with his uncle. Then Uncle Jack came in and said "Don't get a fright. There is a soldier at the door."' The soldier had come from Fermoy, where Ceannt's elder brother William, who would die on the Western Front on the first anniversary of the Rising, was stationed as an army quartermaster. William had asked the soldier, who was on leave, to get news of his brother's fate. That fate was still apparently uncertain.

At about ten o'clock that night an army officer arrived with a note from Eamonn asking Áine and his brothers and sisters to come and see him. 'It was a night of fierce rain, and as we travelled along accompanied by a policeman we came across various patrols, where the policeman put his head out and shouted "Command car. King's Messenger." Notwithstanding all this we were held up on several occasions, and the army officer complained to some of the patrols that they were not standing out where they could be seen, and that some of the men had been fired on during the week.'

Michael O'Hanrahan, who was second in command of the garrison at Jacob's factory, and was executed on May 4th. His family had been told to come to the jail that day to see him 'before his deportation to England'.

THE EXECUTIONS

In all, 16 men were executed for their parts in the Rising and related events.

In Kilmainham Gaol, Dublin:
- May 3rd: Patrick Pearse, Thomas Clarke, Thomas MacDonagh

- May 4th: Ned Daly, Willie Pearse, Michael O'Hanrahan, Joseph Plunkett

- May 5th: John MacBride

- May 8th: Seán Heuston, Michael Mallin, Eamonn Ceannt, Con Colbert

- May 12th: Seán MacDermott, James Connolly

In Cork Detention Barracks:
- May 9th: Thomas Kent (for the murder of Head Constable Rowe of the RIC)

- In Pentonville Prison, London August 3rd: Sir Roger Casement (for high treason)

Major John MacBride had not been a member of the Irish Volunteers at the beginning of the Rising, but offered his services to Thomas MacDonagh's garrison at Jacob's. Not appreciating that he would be executed, while in jail he was worried about losing his Dublin Corporation job.

Michael Collins in the uniform of the Irish Volunteers. Not one of the leaders of the Rising, he spent the week in the GPO and later rose to prominence while in Frongoch internment camp in Wales.

When she got to Kilmainham, her husband was in a different cell, with a few boards to sleep on, a soap box, a chair, a candle, and writing materials. Soldiers were coming in and out and some tried to cheer her up 'saying such things as "It's a long way to Tipperary" and "You never know what will happen."' But Eamonn was feeling the stress of not knowing for sure what his fate would be, whether he would be executed or reprieved. 'Eamonn said his mind had been disturbed. He said "I was quite prepared to walk out of this at a quarter to four in the morning [to be executed], but all this [uncertainty] has upset me."' As they were leaving the prison, Eamonn's youngest brother, Richard, spoke to a senior officer, who told him 'There is no reprieve. Go back and tell your brother.' Richard did not tell Áine about this conversation.

Áine Ceannt stayed up all night praying. At 6am, when the curfew was lifted, she went to the Capuchin priory at Church Street and asked for Fr Augustine, who ministered to many of the executed men. Fr Augustine had just gone up to his room, having come back from an execution. A priest offered to go and fetch him. 'I said no, that I only wanted to know the truth, and this priest said "He is gone to Heaven."' Later that morning, she spoke to Fr Augustine himself, who told her that her husband's last words were 'My Jesus, mercy'. After this conversation 'my sister-in-law suggested that we go and purchase some mourning. As the War was raging at the time and there were many young widows, it was easy to procure an outfit.'

THEN AND NOW: HOW NAMES HAVE CHANGED

- Sackville Street is now O'Connell Street.

- The Imperial Hotel is now part of Clery's department store, O'Connell Street.

- The Metropole Hotel is now Penney's store in O'Connell Street.

- Hopkins jewellers was until recently a building society at the corner of O'Connell Street and Eden Quay.

- Great Brunswick Street is now Pearse Street.

- The South Dublin Union is now St James's Hospital.

- Jervis Street Hospital is now the Jervis Centre in Mary Street.

- Mercer's Hospital was between Grafton Street and South Great George's Street, close to the Stephen's Green Centre.

- Sir Patrick Dun's Hospital was on Lower Grand Canal Street.

- Boland's mill was at Ringsend Road, close to Grand Canal Dock.

- Jacob's Biscuit factory, Bishop Street, was where DIT and the National Archives are now.

- Linen Hall Barracks were on Constitution Hill, near North King Street.

- Richmond Barracks were in Inchicore. St Michael's CBS occupies part of the site.

- Royal Barracks, later known as Collins Barracks, is now part of the National Museum of Ireland.

- The Royal Military Hospital was at Arbour Hill.

- Ship Street Barracks adjoined Dublin Castle.

- Military Headquarters were in Infirmary Road, within the Phoenix Park.

- Wellington Barracks, later Griffith Barracks, now houses Griffith College.

- Harcourt Street Station was the large building beside the Harcourt Luas stop.

- Westland Row Station is now Pearse Station.

- *The Irish Times* offices were on Westmoreland Street, with the printing works behind, on approximately the site occupied by the newspaper until 2006. There was also a 'reserve printing office' at 4 Lower Abbey Street.

Irish nationalism became far more popular after the executions than it had been at any time during the rebellion. These women are pictured holding the tricolour at a mass-meeting in June 1916.

Except for those of the leaders, the trials were often very short, with 36 courts martial held on May 4th alone. William Cosgrave's lasted less than 15 minutes before he was sentenced to death. Even though the proceedings were often rushed and formulaic, however, those charged were seldom in a position to contest the broad thrust of the charges. As Cosgrave acknowledged, 'there was probably not one "innocent" man brought up for Courtmartial'. It was not surprising, in the circumstances, that the courts martial found that all but 11 of the 187 people tried were guilty as charged.

Paradoxically perhaps, relations between the legal and military officials on the one side and the rebel leaders on the other were often characterised by decency and

Mr Justice Shearman attends the Royal Commission on the 1916 Rising, which investigated the events leading up to the rebellion.

kindness. According to Cosgrave, 'the members of the Courtmartial were pleasantly polite. Their knowledge of law was most elementary, so that the Crown Prosecutor had on several occasions to insist upon prisoner's rights.' The deputy advocate-general, William Wylie, also tried to ensure that the trials adopted fair procedures, arguing unsuccessfully that they should be held in public and the prisoners should have defence counsel. The attorney general, James Campbell, rejected Wylie's arguments and told him that 'he wouldn't be satisfied unless 40 of them were shot'. Wylie nonetheless was determined to defend the prisoners' rights and 'bring out every damn thing I could in their favour'.

THE WITNESSES: POSTSCRIPT

Augustine Birrell resigned as chief secretary for Ireland after the Rising and did not contest his seat in the 1918 general election.

Eamon Bulfin's death sentence was commuted because he was born in Argentina. Deported to Buenos Aires, he was jailed for deserting military service there. Released in 1919, he co-ordinated fundraising and arms shipments from there until he returned to Ireland in 1922.

Áine Ceannt was vice-president of Cumann na mBan from 1917 to 1925, and as an anti-Treaty activist was jailed in Mountjoy for a year during the Civil War. She was later a founding member of the Irish Red Cross.

William T. Cosgrave was sentenced to death for his role in the Rising, but that was commuted to penal servitude for life; he was released in 1918. In 1922 he became president of the Irish Free State.

Capt. Arthur Annan Dickson was sent to France in 1917. A commander of a Trench Mortar Battery, he was shot through the neck in 1918. Demobilised from the army, he became a bank manager. He also became a Quaker and pacifist, and the pocket book that saved his life – with the bullet still lodged in it – is kept in the Imperial War Museum.

Capt. E. Gerrard continued to serve in the British Army, and was stationed in Ireland during the War of Independence, and later served as far afield as Somaliland.

Arthur and Mary Louisa Hamilton Norway both wrote memoirs about the Rising. She died in 1932; he in 1938. Their son, Nevil, acted as a stretcher bearer during the Rising and (as Nevil Shute) became a bestselling author.

Robert Holland was imprisoned at Knutsford Prison in Cheshire until August, after which he was transferred to Frongoch internment camp in Wales.

John Joly held his professorship in Trinity until 1933, the year of his death. In 1973, a Martian crater was named after him.

General Sir John Grenfell Maxwell returned to England later in 1916. After being stationed in Egypt, he retired in 1922 and died in 1929.

Helena Molony was imprisoned for several months after the Rising. She actively opposed the Treaty during the Civil War. She later became a leading trade unionist.

Sir Matthew Nathan moved back to the British ministry of pensions, and in 1920 became governor of Queensland until retirement in 1925.

Elizabeth O'Farrell spent several months in prison after the Rising. She died in 1957. A Nurse Elizabeth O'Farrell Foundation was set up to support postgraduate studies in the field of nursing.

Ernie O'Malley later became a leading republican figure, and was active in raids against British troops until he was jailed, and then escaped, in 1921. Anti-Treaty during the Civil War, he was badly wounded and then jailed. He became a writer, best known for his account of the War of Independence, *On Another Man's Wound*.

James Stephens was registrar of the National Gallery of Ireland until 1924 and continued to be a prolific writer after he moved to England in 1925. His *Irish Fairy Tales* is considered a classic.

Joseph Sweeney was imprisoned in England and Wales after the Rising, and later became a Sinn Féin TD. He fought in the Free State army during the Civil War and later became the Army's chief of staff.

Active in both the War of Independence, and on the anti-Treaty side of the Civil War, **Oscar Traynor** became a TD and minister for defence. He was also a president of the Football Association of Ireland.

Thomas Walsh and his brother **James** remained on the run from the authorities until Christmas. Their account is included in the Bureau of Military History archives.

Martin Walton was later involved in the War of Independence before going on to become a leading figure in Irish music, setting up the Dublin College of Music and a well-known music retail business.

Lord Wimborne was lord-lieutenant until 1918, after which he was made Viscount Wimborne.

Held in Wakefield Military Detention prison, **Dick Humphreys** wrote a book, *Easter Week in the GPO*, on prison toilet paper. Jailed during the War of Independence he later rode in the Isle of Man TT and set up an automobile parts shop in Dublin.

Ms Louisa Nolan, one of the many women to have been involved in the Easter Rising, at a ceremony in February 1917 at which she received a military medal for her actions during Easter week.

Capt. H.V. Stanley, an Irish Protestant and an officer in the Royal Army Medical Corps, looked after wounded prisoners who were being held at Dublin Castle. According to Father Aloysius, a Capuchin friar who tended to their religious needs, Stanley 'said it would be a consolation if one of the priests would drop into the "Sinn Féin" ward in which the other prisoner-patients were, and say a word to those in it, and let their friends know that they were alive … I was permitted to go round to each bed and speak to the patients. Some of them said they would be grateful if I would send them prayer-books. Captain Stanley said he would distribute them with pleasure if I sent them; and he did very kindly distribute the books which were sent ... Captain Stanley showed himself, all through, a Christian and humane man, and James Connolly spoke to me of his very great kindness to him, although Stanley was politically and in religion at variance with the prisoners ...'

J.C. Ridgway, a Waterford-born doctor in the Royal Medical Corps, who had been at the Fairyhouse races when the Rising broke out, tended to James Connolly in Dublin Castle. 'Twice daily I dressed the wound and had little chats with him so I naturally got attached to my patient.

'When dressing his leg one evening I said in a low voice: "Is there anything I could do for you in a small way?" He looked surprised and on my repeating the question, he said; "Yes, I would like to get a message to my wife." As far as I can now recollect he was given notepaper, an envelope and a pencil and a message was sent and a reply came back.'

Eamonn Ceannt noted of his jailers on the day before his execution that 'all here are very kind' and his last words, according to the priest who witnessed his execution, were 'telling of the kindness of a British officer'. One member of the firing squad who shot Con Colbert pinned the regulation white square above his heart 'and then added "Give me your hand now." The prisoner seemed confused and extended his left hand. "Not that," said the soldier, but the right." The right was accordingly extended, and having shaken it warmly, the kindly-human-hearted soldier proceeded to bind gently the prisoner's hands behind his back, and afterwards blindfolded him.'

All of the executions were carried out in the Stonebreaker's Yard in Kilmainham. General Maxwell had decided that the bodies would not be given for burial to the families of the dead men: 'Irish sentimentality

WINNER ALL SORTS

The 1916 Irish Grand National was run on Easter Monday in Fairyhouse and won by all sorts. A horse with the rather apt name of 'Civil War' also ran in the race, but didn't feature.

A Free State commemoration at Kilmainham, marking an anniversary of the Rising and the execution of its leaders.

would turn those graves into martyrs' shrines to which annual processions etc. will be made … the executed rebels are to be buried in quicklime, without coffins.' These orders were carried out, and the bodies were buried in quicklime in Arbour Hill Barracks.

For those who were involved in carrying out the executions, military procedures attempted to make the bloody business as routine as possible. Arthur Dickson, who commanded one of the firing squads, remembered: 'A kindly but strict old Major of one of the other Battalions gave detailed instructions to each of us: I was to march my firing-squad of a Sergeant and twelve men to a space cut off from the execution-point by a projecting wall; halt them to ground arms there; march them forward twelve paces to halt with their backs to their rifles each of which I was then to load and replace on the ground. Thus no man knew whether his rifle had been loaded with black or with ball; each was therefore left not knowing whether he personally had shot the man or not.'

'The men were then marched back to pick up their rifles and hold them, at attention under my eye, until word came that the prisoner was to be led out; they must then be marched round and halted facing the execution wall.

'We marched our squads to [Kilmainham] Prison long before dawn in a dismal drizzle, but the men with memories of our losses seemed to have no qualms as to doing the job. "Pity to dirty all these rifles; why can't we do him in with a bit of bayonet practice?" We had to wait while it grew faintly light and I took the chance to instruct the squad exactly what orders they would get; I didn't want any muddle about getting them back around that wall … Thanks to that preparation, it was carried out smoothly. The thirteen rifles went off in a single volley. The rebel dropped to the ground like an empty sack; I barked out "Slope – ARMS; About – TURN; Quick – MARCH." They marched in perfect order round that wall, grounded arms, and I told them "Right: you made a good job of that, gentlemen"; remember, we had all lost some good pals in our first days' active service. I can't say I felt much else except that it was just another job that had to be done; though I was glad there was no doubt the rifles had done their work and there was no need for me to do what that old Major had told me, about the officer going back and finishing the job off with his revolver.'

Dickson's squad may have been unusually efficient, however, and some of the executions seem to have been more grisly. Áine Ceannt was told by Fr Augustine, who attended many of the executions, that 'in every case it would appear as if it were necessary for the officer in charge of the firing party to dispatch the victim by a revolver shot'. Capt. E. Gerrard subsequently spoke to Capt. H.V. Stanley, who told him 'I was the Medical Officer who attended the executions of the first nine Sinn Féiners to be shot. After that I got so sick of the slaughter that I asked to be changed. Three refused to have their eyes bandaged ... The rifles of the firing party were waving like a field of corn. All the men were cut to ribbons at a range of about ten yards.'

While the army was dealing with its prisoners, it was also trying to restore order to the streets of Dublin which remained, in the immediate aftermath of the Rising, somewhat anarchic. Dickson recalled that 'We captured several Dublin underworld characters looting damaged shops; once we advanced on a considerable crowd threatening this and other damage ... Captain Cooper, after warning the crowd to disperse, ordered me to fire one shot over their heads. I did so, taking careful aim at the girders of a railway bridge across the street beyond them, and they quickly disappeared. Another evening, clearing the streets after curfew, we were defied by an elderly harridan belatedly leaving a porter-shop; evidently expert in resisting the Dublin Police she was a handful for two of our men until I told them to show her their bayonets; she went before them at once to the police Station. "You've got a nice way with the ladies," Cooper remarked.'

By the end of May, martial law, executions and deportations were having a palpable effect on public opinion. General Maxwell himself recognised, as he wrote to his wife that 'a revulsion of feeling has set in'. What he felt was a campaign of misrepresentation had created an exaggerated sense of victimhood. 'Ireland is groaning under the tyranny of martial law. It is all eyewash for so far they have not felt it. But all the cranks and faddists scream before they are hurt ... Every rebel that was killed in Dublin they now say was murdered by soldiers in cold blood.' On June 1st he confessed to his wife that 'I am getting dead sick of this job. I will be the best hated man wherever there are Irish.'

The executions and deportations created an ambiguity even among those mainstream nationalists who strongly opposed the Rising. At first, much respectable opinion was evidently appalled by what had happened. *The Galway Express*, for example, in its leader of April 29th, wrote that 'Easter Monday 1916 has made history in Ireland. But, oh what rank nauseating stains will besmear its pages! – how generations yet unborn will burn with shame when, in the calm light of detailed and exalted impartiality they scan its humiliating chapters!'

Éamon de Valera speaking to a crowd in 1917. The only leader not to be executed, he would go on to become a dominant figure in Irish political life for the next half a century.

Over the next month, though, establishment opinion became more ambivalent. On May 29th, Meath County Council debated a motion which had been forwarded it to it from Tullamore Urban District Council, 'that this council desires to record their outrage at the recent deplorable outbreak in Dublin which they believe to be greatly detrimental to the real industrial and political interests of Ireland'. The motion was passed but so was an amendment to add: 'That we respectfully request the government to deal in a lenient manner with the prisoners now in custody, who through youth or ignorance were the dupes of men who should have known better.'

Like the county councils and the main newspapers, the Catholic hierarchy had initially taken a strongly negative view of the Rising. While some prelates maintained a discreet silence, those who spoke out (seven in all) were extremely hostile to the rebels. The Bishop of Ross denounced their 'senseless, meaningless debauchery of blood'. The Bishop of Kerry described them as 'evil-minded men afflicted by Socialistic and Revolutionary doctrines'. The Bishop of Killaloe lamented 'the mad adventure'.

But gradually, as descriptions of the last days of the leaders began to emerge in publications such as the *Catholic Bulletin*, the men were transformed from dangerous fanatics to Catholic martyrs.

For many of the prisoners, including the Marxist James Connolly, a fervent Catholicism provided consolation in dark times. 'While in Richmond Barracks,' remembered William Cosgrave, "prisoners'" quarters were locked up at 8pm. Shortly after that the Rosary was recited and everyone settled down for the night ... John MacBride told me on one of those nights that his life-long prayer had been answered. He said three Hail Marys every day that he should not die until he had fought the British in Ireland.' In his cell in Arbour Hill Barracks, Patrick Pearse wrote a poem in the voice of his own mother, comparing himself to Christ: 'Dear Mary, that didst see thy first-born Son/ Go forth to die amid the scorn of men/ For whom He died/ Receive my first-born son into thy arms,/ Who has also gone out to die for men ...'

An election poster for Éamon de Valera in the 1923 election, which followed a bloody Civil War and continued debate over who could lay proper claim to the legacy of the 1916 Rising.

Veterans of the 1916 Rising at an event at UCD, 1966.

On the night before Pearse's execution, the Capuchin friar, Fr Aloysius, ministered to him: 'I can never forget the devotion with which he received the Most Blessed Sacrament. I could not help picturing to myself a scene in the Catacombs in the days of the persecutions in Rome. The bare cell was lighted from a candle at a small opening in the cell wall, and I had barely light to read the ritual. But the face of the man, as he lifted it up to receive his God, seemed to beam with light.'

A document that began to circulate in Dublin in June purporting to be Thomas MacDonagh's address to his court martial (its provenance is unclear, but MacDonagh's son accepted that it was probably genuine) had the same air of religious exaltation. He purportedly told the court that he and his colleagues belonged to the 'great unnumbered army of martyrs whose Captain is the Christ who died on Calvary … The forms of heroes flit before my vision, and there is one, the star of whose destiny sways my own; there is one the keynote of whose nature chimes harmoniously with the swan-song of my soul. It is the great Florentine, whose weapon was not the sword but prayer and preaching.' This was a reference to the Benedictine monk Savonarola, who was burned at the stake for leading a revolt in Renaissance Florence, and to whom MacDonagh was devoted.

Amid this religious fervour, it was easy to forget that MacDonagh and his comrades had even borne arms. The Belfast-born playwright and critic St John Ervine, who was manger of the Abbey theatre, recorded that 'When the news of his execution was proclaimed, a woman wept in the street. "Ah, poor Tom MacDonagh," she said. "And he wouldn't have hurt a fly!"'

The religious context of the shift in public mood was reinforced by the memorial Masses for the executed men that began to be celebrated in early June. Todd Andrews, who was then 14, recalled that 'The first open manifestation of the deep public feeling aroused by the executions was at the Month's Mind for the dead leaders. A Month's Mind is the Mass celebrated for the soul of a relative or friend a month after his death. It was the first opportunity that sympathisers of the rebels had to come out in the open. I went with my father to the first of the Month's Minds, which was for the brothers Pearse, at Rathfarnham. We arrived in time for the Mass but could not get into the church and the forecourt was packed right out to the road. I was surprised to see so many well-dressed and obviously well-to-do people present … I went to the other Month's Minds without my father – to Merchant's Quay, John's Lane and other city churches. For us young people these Masses were occasions for quite spontaneous demonstrations, shouting insults at the Dublin Metropolitan Police. We jeered at the "separation women" with their Union Jacks.'

In the public mind, too, the scale of the destruction in Dublin and of the arrests made after the Rising, created a tendency to exaggerate the number of rebels, drawing attention away from their real position as a small and unrepresentative minority. James Stephens wrote that 'No person in Ireland seems to have exact information about the Volunteers, their aims or their numbers. We know the names of the leaders now. They were recited to us with the tale of their execution; and with the declaration of the Republic we learned something of their aim, but the estimate of their number runs through the figures ten, thirty, and fifty thousand. The first figure is undoubtedly too slender, the last excessive, and something between fifteen and twenty thousand for all Ireland would be a reasonable guess.' In fact, even the lowest of these estimates exaggerated the number of Volunteers who participated in the Rising almost by a factor of ten.

An emerging popular cult of the dead heroes, combined with fierce opposition to the threatened introduction of conscription, gradually handed the political initiative to a reconstituted Sinn Féin, which was boosted by the false but almost universal description of the Rising as the Sinn Féin Rebellion. When the opportunity came to contest a parliamentary seat in Roscommon after the death of the Irish Party MP, James O'Kelly, Sinn Féin chose a candidate who copperfastened the fusion of the religious and the political in its new identity. George Noble Plunkett was both father of the executed Joseph Plunkett and a papal count. He easily defeated the Irish Party candidate in the election in February 1917.

Just over a year after the Rising, in May 1917, the reconstituted executive of the Irish Volunteers, including Michael Collins, who had been in the GPO during Easter Week, issued a new manifesto. It ordered Volunteers not to obey any instructions that did not come from the executive – an order that would have prevented the Rising itself from taking place.

And, in a further implicit rebuke to the tactics of the rebel leaders, it guaranteed that the executive would 'not issue an order to take to the field until they consider that the force is in a position to wage war on the enemy with reasonable hopes of success. Volunteers as a whole may consequently rest assured that they will not be called upon to take part in any forlorn hope.' The message was clear: the Rising was to be revered but not to be repeated.

A few months later, the poet, painter and organiser of agricultural co-operatives George Russell wrote a poem looking back on the deaths in violent conflict of six men he knew: Patrick Pearse, Thomas MacDonagh and James Connolly, executed after the Rising, and Alan Anderson, Thomas Kettle and Willie Redmond, killed on the Western Front. He ended it by imagining all of them, and all of the other dead Irishmen,

> Thronged on some starry parapet,
> That looks down upon Innisfail,
> And sees the confluence of dreams
> That clashed together in our night.
> One river, born from many streams,
> Roll in one blaze of blinding light.

THE PROCLAMATION

There is a mystery about who wrote the Proclamation. It is assumed that Patrick Pearse wrote a draft, with additions by James Connolly and other signatories, but nobody knows for certain. The opening lines with their appeal to history have the ring of Pearse about them while the later reference to the right of the people of Ireland to the ownership of Ireland sounds like Connolly.

The document itself was printed in Liberty Hall the day before the Rising started. About 2,500 copies were run off on the presses that produced Connolly's *Workers' Republic* newspaper. Pearse read the Proclamation to a crowd of onlookers outside the GPO on Easter Monday and copies were posted up in the street or left around to be taken away by onlookers.

It is believed that about 40 copies of the original Proclamation still exist. One is on display in Leinster House, another in the National Library while the National Museum acquired one in 2006. In 2004 one was sold at auction for €390,000.

Watching from the balcony of the Metropole Hotel as Pearse read the Proclamation outside the GPO, L.G. Redmond-Howard, a nephew of John Redmond, noted that some members of the crowd took away copies as souvenirs as 'they'd be worth a fiver each some day, when the beggars were hanged'.

BIBLIOGRAPHY

Barton, Brian and Foy, Michael: *The Easter Rising* (Gloucestershire, 1999)

Caulfield, Max: *The Easter Rebellion* (London, 1995)

Collins, Lorcan and Kostick, Conor: *The Easter Rising: A Guide to Dublin in 1916* (Dublin, 1996)

Coogan, Tim Pat: *1916: The Easter Rising* (London, 2001)

Dudley Edwards, Owen and Pyle, Fergus (eds.): *1916: The Easter Rising* (London, 1968)

Ebenezer, Lyn: *Frongoch and the Birth of the IRA* (Llanwrst, 2005)

Findlater, Alex: *Findlaters: The Story of a Dublin Merchant Family* (Dublin, 2001)

Griffith, Kenneth and O'Grady, Timothy: *Curious Journey: An Oral History of Ireland's Unfinished Revolution* (Dublin, 1998)

Jeffrey, Keith: *The GPO and the Easter Rising* (Dublin, 2006)

Kain, R.: 'A Diary of Easter Week: One Dubliner's Experience', in *Irish University Review*, 10 (1980)

Lynch, Diarmuid: *The IRB and the 1916 Insurrection* (Cork, 1957)

McGuiggan, John: 'In Some Forgotten Corner of a Foreign Field' (*www.crich-memorial.org.uk/foreignfield.html*)

McHugh, Roger: *Dublin 1916* (London, 1966)

Mac Lochlainn, Piaras: *Last Words* (Dublin, 1971)

Martin, F.X. (ed.): *Leaders and Men of the Easter Rising: Dublin 1916* (Dublin, 1967)

Nic Dhonnachadha, Máirín and Dorgan, Theo (eds.): *Revising the Rising* (Derry, 1991)

Nowlan, K.B. (ed.): *The Making of 1916* (Dublin, 1969)

Ó Broin, Leon: *Dublin Castle and the 1916 Rising* (London, 1966)

Ó Broin, Leon: *The Chief Secretary: Augustine Birrell in Ireland* (London, 1969)

Stephens, James: *The Insurrection in Dublin* (Dublin, 1965)

Taillon, Ruth: *The Women of 1916* (Belfast, 1996)

Townshend, Charles: *Easter 1916: The Irish Rebellion* (London, 2005)

FURTHER READING:

Leaders

(a) Patrick Pearse

Connolly O'Brien, Nora: 'The Pearse I knew', in *Hibernia*, April 15th 1977

Dudley Edwards, Ruth: *Patrick Pearse: The Triumph of Failure* (London, 1977)

Maguire, Desmond (ed.): *Short Stories of Padraic Pearse: A Dual-Language Book* (Dublin and Cork, 1998)

Ó Buachalla, Séamus (ed.): *The Literary Writings of Patrick Pearse* (Dublin and Cork, 1979)

Ó Buachalla, Séamus (ed.): *A Significant Irish Educationalist: The Educational Writings of P.H. Pearse* (Dublin and Cork, 1980)

Ryan, Desmond: *The Man Called Pearse* (Dublin, 1919)

Sisson, Elaine: *Pearse's Patriots: St Enda's and the Cult of Boyhood* (Cork, 2005)

(b) James Connolly

Beresford Ellis, Peter (ed.): *James Connolly: Selected Writings* (London, 1997)

Connolly O'Brien, Nora: *Portrait of a Rebel Father* (Dublin, 1935)

Dudley Edwards, Ruth: *James Connolly* (Dublin, 1981)

Fox, R.M.: *James Connolly: The Forerunner* (Tralee, 1946)

Mac an Bheatha, Proinsias: *Tart na Córa: Seamus Ó Conghaile, A Shaol agus A Shaothar* (Baile Átha Cliath, dáta ar bith)

Nevin, Donal: *Connolly Bibliography* (Dublin, ICTU, 1968)

Nevin, Donal: *James Connolly: 'A Full Life'* (Dublin, 2005)

Ryan, Desmond: *James Connolly: His Life, Work and Writings* (Dublin, 1924)

(c) Joseph Plunkett

MacDonagh, Donagh: 'Plunkett and MacDonagh', in F.X. Martin (ed.): *Leaders and Men*

Plunkett, Geraldine (ed.): *The Poems of Joseph Mary Plunkett* (Dublin, 1919) available on
www.poetry.elcore.net/CathPoets/Plunkett

(d) Thomas MacDonagh

The Poetical Works of Thomas MacDonagh (Dublin, 1919)

Norstedt, J.A.: *Thomas MacDonagh* (Charlottesville, North Carolina, 1980)

(e) Seán MacDermott

MacAtasney, Gerard: *Seán Mac Diarmada: Mind of the Revolution* (Manorhamilton, 2004)

(f) Eamonn Ceannt

Henry, William: *Supreme Sacrifice: The Story of Eamonn Ceannt* (Dublin, 2005)

(g) Thomas J. Clarke

Le Roux, Louis: *Tom Clarke and the Irish Freedom Movement* (Dublin, 1926)

Other participants

Bourke, Marcus: *The O'Rahilly* (Tralee, 1967)

FitzGerald, Desmond: *The Memoirs of Desmond FitzGerald 1913–1916* (London, 1968)

Haverty, Ann: *Constance Markievicz: An Independent Life* (London, 1988)

Inglis, Brian: *Roger Casement* (London, 1993)

Jordan, Anthony: *Major John MacBride: MacDonagh and MacBride, Connolly and Pearse* (Westport, 1991)

Levenson, Leah: *With Wooden Sword: A Portrait of Francis Sheehy Skeffington* (Boston and Dublin, 1983)

Marreco, Anne: *The Rebel Countess: The Life of Constance Markievicz* (Dublin, 1967)

Norman, Diana: *Terrible Beauty: A Life of Constance Markievicz 1868–1927* (London, 1987)

Ó Briain, Liam: *Cuimhní Cinn* (Baile Átha Cliath, 1951)

Ó hAnnracháin, Peadar: *Mar Mhaireas É* (Baile Átha Cliath, 1953)

O'Neill, Marie: *Grace Gifford Plunkett and Irish Freedom: Tragic Bride of 1916* (Dublin, 2000)

O'Rahilly, Aodogán: *Winding the Clock: O'Rahilly and the 1916 Rising* (Dublin, 1991)

O'Sullivan, Michael and Ó Síocháin, Séamus (eds.): *The Eyes of Another Race: Roger Casement's Congo Report and 1903 Diary* (London, 2004)

Tierney, Michael: *Eoin MacNeill: Scholar and Man of Action* (Oxford, 1980)

Valiulis, Maryann: *Portrait of a Revolutionary: General Richard Mulcahy* (Kentucky, 1992)

Literary

Curtayne, Alice: *The Complete Poems of Francis Ledwidge* (Dublin, 1998)

Kettle, Tom: 'To my daughter, Betty, the gift of God'

Ledwidge, Francis: 'Lament for Thomas MacDonagh'

McGuinness, Frank: *Observe the Sons of Ulster* in *Plays One* (London, 1996)

Ryan, Desmond: *The 1916 Poets* (Dublin, 1963)

Thompson, W.I.: *The Imagination of an Insurrection, Dublin, Easter 1916* (New York, 1967)

Yeats, W.B.: 'Easter 1916'

Visual

Insurrection (RTÉ Libraries and Archives)

Irish Destiny (Irish Film Institute)

The 1916 Rebellion Walking Tour (*www.1916rising.com*)

Irish National War Memorial, Islandbridge, Dublin (Office of Public Works)

Garden of Remembrance, Parnell Square, Dublin (Office of Public Works)

Mise Éire (Gael Linn)

Museums, etc.

Kilmainham Gaol, Dublin 8 (Office of Public Works)

National Museum of Ireland – Decorative Arts & History (Collins Barracks): exhibition, The Easter Rising: Understanding 1916

INDEX

(Note: page numbers in italics refer to illustrations and captions)

THE 1916 RISING

PREFACE

Easter came late in 1916. Although Nationalist sentiment in Ireland had been making its presence felt and there had been a show of strength by armed men marching on the streets of Dublin on St Patrick's Day. There was little sense of what was to happen. The weather was fine. With the Irish Grand National at Fairyhouse on Easter Monday and the Spring Show about to begin at Ballsbridge, most citizens were preparing to enjoy a spring break. The events which were about to unfold told a different story.

Easter Sunday April 23rd

Manoeuvres by the Irish Volunteers and the Citizen Army, planned as a cover for the beginning of the Rising, are cancelled by the Volunteers' chief of staff, Eoin MacNeill. Large numbers of rebels gather in Dublin and around the country, but there is deep confusion about what is to happen. The rebel leaders decide to postpone the Rising until noon on Monday. Explosives are stolen by the rebels and stored in Liberty Hall (1). The authorities discuss a plan to raid Liberty Hall and arrest and deport the rebel leaders but decide to put off action until Monday at the earliest.

Easter Monday April 24th

The rebels turn out in reduced numbers in Dublin and begin their operations at noon, seizing the General Post Office (2), Boland's Mill (3), The South Dublin Union (now St James's Hospital) (4), Jacob's factory in Bishop Street (5) and other buildings. The rebels fail to capture the largely undefended centre of the administration at Dublin Castle but occupy the adjacent City Hall (6) instead. Patrick Pearse reads the Proclamation of the Irish Republic outside the GPO. Transport and distribution services break down throughout the city. Large-scale looting begins in the Sackville Street (now O'Connell Street) area. During the night, government troops quietly take over the Shelbourne Hotel (7), occupying a commanding position overlooking the Citizen Army positions in Stephen's Green.

Tuesday April 25th

Government forces arrive in the city by train overnight from Belfast and the Curragh. Machine gun fire from the roof of the Shelbourne Hotel forces the rebels to leave their positions in Stephen's Green and withdraw

into the College of Surgeons (8). Government troops retake City Hall and the nearby offices of the *Daily Express*. The deranged Captain Bowen-Colthurst arrests three innocent civilians, including the pacifist Francis Sheehy Skeffington, and has them shot the next morning.

Wednesday April 26

At 8am, the shelling of an empty Liberty Hall begins. Rebels holding out in the Mendicity Institute (9), near the Four

tion finally runs out. British troops continue landing at Kingstown (now Dun Laoghaire). The public welcome soldiers by giving them food as they march towards the city. At Mount Street Bridge (11) rebels engage these troops. In a battle that lasts until evening, there are heavy British casualties. Fires begin to spread on O'Connell Street. General Sir John Grenfell Maxwell is despatched from London to deal with the Rising.

Thursday April 27

In the GPO James Connolly is wounded. At the Four Courts and North King Street (12) rebels